PSYCHOLOGY
for everyone

Blanca Pelayo

TRAZO EDITORIAL

México

CONTENTS

INTRODUCTION

What is the first thing that comes to mind when you hear the word "psychology"? Someone experimenting on animals in a lab? A person in a white lab coat treating patients in a psychiatric hospital? A man with glasses and a beard who is "psychoanalyzing" a patient lying on a couch? A charlatan trying to read minds in order to manipulate them?

Psychology is undoubtedly one of the sciences that attracts the most curiosity. And while many of the concepts and terms used in psychology are increasingly common in everyday culture, a significant number of people have only a vague idea of what psychologists do.

Although the initial questions reflect stereotypes that do not necessarily correspond to reality, the confusion is understandable. This is partly due to the fact that psychology has a relatively recent history as a science, unlike ancient sciences such as mathematics, physics, astronomy, or medicine.

Psychology is a broad field that influences many aspects of our lives, including politics, education, art, sports, music, marketing, business, and personal relationships. Ignoring the psychological perspective would hinder our understanding of the world.

But it has not always been this way. Psychology became

a formal science in 1879 with the establishment of the first laboratory for experimental psychology by Wilhelm Wundt, a German physician. The creation of this laboratory opened new paths in previously unexplored research areas. Psychology has shifted its focus over time from exclusively studying the brain, memory, learning, or abnormality to being more interested in how feelings determine our behaviors, how we perceive reality, make decisions, or influence the behavior of others.

It was precisely the interest in human behavior that led me to study psychology and subsequently write about this fascinating science. After nearly a decade of collaborating with monthly publications, I compiled the most discussed topics by readers and provided them with concepts, principles, and tools that have worked in psychotherapy with my patients; some of their cases are exemplified in the following pages.

The goal of this book is to bring to your fingertips the topics in psychology that commonly generate interest and attempt to provide answers to some of the questions you may have asked yourself: Why do I feel like my life is boring? Why do I struggle to finish tasks? Why do I feel like I am not good enough? Can I control my thoughts? Why do I often get sick? Why am I not satisfied with life? Why do I feel unhappy with my body? Is my fear rational or a phobia? Why do I find it difficult to empathize with others? Why do I jump to the wrong conclusions? Why do I wait for others to take the initiative? Why do others dislike me? Why is gender dysphoria on the rise among young people? and many more... If you are also interested in understanding the concept of psychological projection, if your dreams can predict your future, if hypnosis works or if it is "brainwashing", if you are being manipulated by subliminal messages, if a relative or friend is a narcissist, why you are judged by others, if you have been ghosted, why you buy what you buy, how addicted you are to your cell phone, why prices in the supermarket end in 0.99, or why the Starbucks logo is green and Coca-Cola's red, then do not hesitate any longer and start reading!

Use psychology to better understand everyday situations, gain insight into your own thought processes, and understand the reasons behind your behaviors. The goal is to develop tools to improve assertiveness, anger management, self-esteem, stress management, emotional regulation, and positive relationships. To summarize, this book will help you achieve mental wellness and find joy in your life.

In short, if you want to understand the reasons why you do what you do, then this book is for you. Explore the mysteries of your mind in a language that is clear and easy to understand.

WHAT DO YOU THINK WHEN YOU LOOK AT YOURSELF IN THE MIRROR?

What do you see when you look in the mirror? Are you satisfied with your physical appearance? Do you smile because you are alive? Do you believe in your abilities and talents? Do you know how to take negative criticism? Do you embrace new challenges with enthusiasm? If your answer is yes, congratulations! You seem to have a healthy self-esteem. If your answer is "no," it's worth reading on.

Self-esteem can be defined as the love we have for ourselves. It is the way we perceive and accept ourselves as valuable beings.

But how is self-esteem built? The process of building self-esteem is not a conscious or voluntary one. Rather, it is formed during childhood through the positive or negative messages received from parents. These messages are internalized and shape our daily attitudes.

Imagine you are a child and your upset mom tells you, 'You are a bad kid,' when she really means, 'I don't like what you're doing.' However, if these messages are consistently repeated, the words 'I am bad' will stay with you, even as you grow up and forget the reason you received that message.

Parental love should be based on the fact that they are their children, rather than on the idea that they are good or do good things. However, young children may not perceive this difference, and may start to believe that they are not good or valuable enough.

According to Erik Erikson's theory of personality development[1], self-esteem formation begins in early life. The degree of trust a child acquires depends on the quality of the maternal relationship. Mothers instill trust in their children by caring for their basic needs. If parents feed, care for, and love their newborn, the child will grow up feeling that the world is a safe place.

On the other hand, a person who did not have their basic needs attended to during childhood, was ignored by their parents or other significant people, or was not sufficiently praised for their actual achievements, may develop a poor self-image. Furthermore, they may perceive the world as a frightening place.

Have you ever heard someone regularly repeat phrases like 'I can't do this,' 'Nothing good ever happens to me,' or 'I can't get anything right'? Psychologists have found that maintaining this incessant and negative internal monologue as a habit can lead to the development of depression.

Individuals with low self-esteem desire happiness but often feel undeserving of it, leading to feelings of guilt for experiencing positive emotions about themselves.

A person with low self-esteem sometimes gives up and feels

powerless, as if they deserve all the bad things that happen to them. This can lead to projecting aggression and violence towards others as a means of coping with their negative self-image. Did you know that people who generally show violence and aggression are often hiding their own frustration?

Individuals with low self-esteem often base their self-worth on external factors, such as the opinions of others. They may seek recognition or praise to feel validated, and criticism can significantly lower their self-esteem. Success can boost their confidence, while failure can lead to feelings of inadequacy.

How can individuals with low self-esteem be identified?

Some traits include pessimism and doubt regarding potentially positive outcomes, harsh self-criticism in the face of failure, extreme sensitivity to criticism from others, a persistent state of boredom, depression, and low enthusiasm, and a lack of humor resulting in a generally sad demeanor. Individuals with these traits may believe that their life lacks meaning or significance, experience a sense of purposelessness, exhibit introverted behavior, struggle to express their feelings and have difficulties socializing.

If you identify with any of these traits, it is important to seek professional help as you may have low self-esteem issues that might otherwise be easily resolved with meaningful counseling and guidance.

One effective method for addressing self-esteem issues is psychotherapy, specifically the cognitive-behavioral model[2]. By working directly with thoughts, this model can be highly effective in improving self-esteem. This approach focuses on identifying negative thought patterns that motivate problematic behaviors. Patients are asked to list their negative thoughts in one column, such as "I can't do anything right", and then provide a positive antidote in another column, such as "I can do things, one at a time". Subsequently, these statements are repeated regularly for a few minutes several times a day. This gradual repetition helps to change negative thought patterns, leading individuals to think more positively about themselves and their lives.

Consider starting today. Make a list of your negative thoughts and replace them with positive affirmations.

Give it a try. You may soon notice a change in the way you perceive yourself.

2

DON'T PUT IT OFF UNTIL TOMORROW...

Did you fail to go to the gym, lose weight, save money, or be on time? What was the last resolution you failed to keep?

As we start a new year, a new job, or a new relationship, we make resolutions we are determined to keep. But after a few weeks, the energy and excitement with which we started out fades away, and we begin to put off the activities or situations that we have set for ourselves, and replace them with ones that are more enjoyable. So, we stop going to the gym because the boss asks us to work overtime, we don't save money because of an irresistible offer to buy a 65-inch screen, or our grades at school don't improve because we join a music band.

Putting things off for later is one of the biggest problems we face at some point in our lives, or in the worst cases, all the time.

Procrastination consists of putting off things that need to be done, delaying anything uncomfortable or unacceptable to us, and replacing it with less important or more enjoyable activities.

The origin of the verb "procrastinate" can be traced to the Latin verb "procrastinare," which means "in regard to tomorrow".

The habit of procrastination can lead to an addiction to various activities, such as surfing the Internet, reading books, shopping, compulsive eating, or getting caught up in the work routine, as an excuse to avoid some responsibility, action, or decision.

Why do we put things off? Because the postponed action may be perceived as boring, difficult, overwhelming, unsettling, challenging, or stressful. That is why it is classified as "for later".

Imagine you have a number of activities that you find less enjoyable or boring (this is often the case with household chores). Which one will you prioritize? Obviously, the one that is the least unpleasant of all, and you will leave the one that causes you the most aversion until last.

If you frequently find yourself caught in the irrational cycle of chronic procrastination, it's not because of a lack of time but rather the difficulty of managing negative moods associated with a task. Procrastination is an emotional issue, not a time management problem.[3]

It is also possible to delay a task because of the fear of successfully completing it. Perhaps you are a perfectionist or fear not meeting certain expectations. Resistance may be linked to deeper feelings related to the task, such as insecurity, anxiety, or low self-esteem. For instance, activities like preparing a presentation or writing an essay can be intimidating if you believe you are not capable enough to express your ideas. Postponing a task may also result from lack of motivation, not finding what you have to do relevant, or struggling with prioritizing your activities and defining what is most important.

Regardless of the reason for procrastination, it is important to remember that your current position in life is a result of your daily habits. As the saying goes, 'your habits predict your future,' and this holds very true.

How to overcome the destructive habit of procrastination?

First, you need to identify what you are putting off. Take a pen and write down the tasks you usually procrastinate on, such as studying for an important exam, submitting a report at work, scheduling a medical appointment, starting a gym routine, and so on.

Now, ask yourself why you are putting off each of these activities. Perhaps you prefer watching television or browsing the internet instead of studying for an exam, or going shopping with your friends instead of going to the gym.

The next step is to imagine yourself five years from now, how your body would look, how much energy and physical fitness you would have, and now imagine what would happen if you decided not to go to the gym and instead gained weight and developed disease. For instance, consider what could happen within those five years if you commit to regularly going to the gym starting today. How would your life be?

Consider saving a percentage of your salary each month instead of taking advantage of all the online shopping deals. You might be able to buy your dream house, upgrade your car to a newer model, or take that trip you've always wanted. Finally, consider the potential consequences of failing the final examination due to insufficient preparation and having to repeat a year of school.

In most cases, procrastination is primarily caused by unpleasant emotions associated with task completion, making it difficult to prioritize them. Therefore, it is important to adjust our activities by focusing on the most important tasks with closer deadlines. By postponing a decision, we are exhibiting evasive behavior, and we may use the phrase 'I'll do it when I have time' as an excuse.

Changing your mindset can help control bad habits. Consider the following ideas:

- Create daily schedules and to-do lists, making sure to stick to them.
- Plan your time by marking all important dates and activities on a calendar or agenda.
- Set deadlines for starting activities and tasks.
- Divide any project into smaller tasks, each taking no more than 20 minutes, and track your progress by marking completed tasks.
- Reward yourself for your achievements.
- Change your mindset from 'I have to do it' to 'I want to do it'.

Motivational speaker and self-help author Tony Robbins[4] says that everything we do in life is either to avoid unpleasant situations or to gain pleasure. We strive to avoid pain in the present moment, not realizing that there may be greater pain in the future: regret.

Remember that the reason you are procrastinating is because you are focusing on what you don't like, instead of focusing on the end results you will get if you do what you should.

Therefore, I invite you to stop thinking about the difficult path you will have to face and focus on what you will gain if you overcome the bad habit of procrastination.

3

HOW TO EXPRESS YOUR FEELINGS

Imagine the following situation: You go to a restaurant for dinner, the waiter brings you what you ordered, and you notice that there is a hair in your soup. This is obviously an inconvenience.

In this situation, you have a few options:

a) You can remove the hair and eat the soup with disgust, or push it aside and not eat it.

b) You can become angry with the waiter and complain loudly.

c) You can call the waiter over, look him in the eye, and politely ask for something else to eat.

You may be familiar with the previous scene, as you may have experienced it personally or witnessed it with someone you know. It may surprise you to learn that most people, in these circumstances, respond according to options *a* and *b*, despite these behaviors being inappropriate for dealing with such a situation.

Those who choose the first option (*passive communication*) decide to avoid conflicts and, in order to not have a bad time, do not honestly express their opinion. They feel uncomfortable eating something that is unpleasant, but are unable to express what they think.

There are also those who respond with *aggressive commu-nication*, feeling entitled to show their anger and loudly demanding better service.

Communicating repeatedly, whether passively or aggressively, makes us dysfunctional in social life and causes discomfort. The middle ground between these two behaviors is assertiveness (*option c*), a mature communication style through which people neither submit to the will of others, but clearly state their opinions and feelings, and firmly advocate for their rights and needs without violating the rights of others.[5]

When someone mistreats you or commits an injustice against you, are you unable to express your discomfort? Are you paralyzed by fear? To make others "respect you," do you react violently and aggressively?

According to psychologists, a healthy expression of our emotions, which they call "*assertiveness*," should move between two extremes. An assertive person clearly and respectfully communicates needs, wants, and feelings while respecting others and standing up for their rights.

The key to achieving assertive behavior is expressing our desires, thoughts, feelings, and needs in a respectful manner without hurting or harming others. Assertiveness values both our opinion as well as that of others.

However, it is more than just saying yes or no. It also involves recognizing positive or negative emotions and being consistent with our verbal and non-verbal expressions. For example, if our face reflects annoyance or anger, it is illogical to verbally agree with someone.

An assertive person can change their mind, admit when they lack knowledge or understanding, acknowledge their mistakes, accept compliments or praise, talk about themselves without hesitation, and express their preferences and interests naturally.

In addition, assertive behaviors are also useful in situations where we feel we are undervalued, whether by a boss, a colleague, a teacher, a partner, or a relative. Assertiveness is also helpful when we need to make a point or get someone to agree to disagree in complex situations.

Assertiveness can be seen as a negotiation. Both parties benefit from an agreement.

A helpful technique for becoming more assertive is to begin by listening to the other person's thoughts without interrupting or judging. This approach helps to prevent opposition from the other person and increases the probability that you will pay attention when it's our turn to speak. This is a good time to express our thoughts objectively on the situation. We can suggest a mutually beneficial solution by using phrases such as 'I propose that...' or 'What if we...'.

Let's consider a scenario where a couple is trying to decide on a movie to see. The woman wants to see a romantic movie, while the man prefers a suspense film that will soon be taken off the schedule. Both insist on their right to choose, and neither is interested in the other's movie choice. To avoid hurting his girlfriend's feelings and to respect both their preferences, the man proposes a solution: "I understand that you want to go see this movie because you like how the lead actress performs, and I chose it last time, but I think it would be better to see the suspense movie because it will leave soon the cinema."

As you can see, negotiation in this case can lead to a win-win agreement because he is expressing what he wants to achieve, why he wants to achieve it, how he wants to achieve it, and how his decision is mutually beneficial.

To increase assertiveness, the first step is to identify situations in which assertiveness is needed. It is important to recognize who the person or situation is with whom we want to be more assertive, to identify the feelings and thoughts that concern us, and then to find a goal and a way to confront the situation.

How to become assertive

First, clearly express your thoughts using the first-person point of view, whether it's a positive or negative feeling. For example: 'When you yell at me, I feel sad' or 'It bothers me when you speak that way.' Additionally, pay attention to your non-verbal language as it can affect how your message is received. Remember to avoid aggressive behavior, even if your words are appropriate.

Avoid making judgments or evaluations about other people's behavior.

Learn to say no without giving further explanations. This avoids turning explanations into justifications and giving the other person the option to try to overturn your decision. For instance, if you cannot or do not want to lend money to someone, avoid justifying it with statements like 'I had a lot of expenses this month' and simply say, 'I cannot lend you money this time.'

Finally, it is important to remember that an assertive person is able to ask, refuse, negotiate, and be flexible to get what they want, always expressing their desires clearly and directly.

④

IS STRESS MAKING YOU SICK?

Have you ever experienced physical pain such as stomach or headache after feeling angry in the morning? While there are various factors that can cause illness, including genetics, environmental factors, and unhealthy habits, we may sometimes experience unexplained headaches or numbness in certain parts of our body. It is important to consider the possibility that these symptoms may be a result of somatizing our emotions, such as sadness or anger, that we experienced earlier in the day

One of the most frequently discussed topics in healthcare is the impact of emotions on physical well-being. It is advisable to listen to our bodies when they communicate through physical discomfort in order to identify and eliminate the root cause.

When considering stressful situations, negative events such as illness, harm, or the death of a loved one often come to mind. However, we are wise to recognize that positive events can likewise be equally stressful, such as moving to a new home or changing jobs, as they require adapting to a new situation. It is equally relevant to acknowledge that stress can arise from both positive and negative events. Even falling in love can be stressful for some people, as can ending a relationship.

Stress is a common occurrence in daily life and can result from any change that requires adaptation. It is a reaction to situations that demand action beyond our capabilities. Stressful experiences have three basic sources: our environment, our body, and our thoughts.[6]

The second source of stress is physiological and is related to how our body reacts during changes such as adolescence, aging, illness, accidents, fear or sleep disorders. When we experience stress, our heart rate increases and we may begin to sweat. These are examples of stress manifestations. However, stress can have more serious consequences, such as fatigue, diabetes, hypertension, ulcers, and increased susceptibility to diseases. For instance, a stressful event like the death of a loved one, job loss, or divorce can lead to high blood pressure or a stomach ulcer.

The stress mechanism previously served the purpose of preparing humans to respond to states of emergency that posed a physical threat. The response to this type of emergency was usually either fleeing or fighting, which required a large amount of energy and muscular strength. The prehistoric humans faced wild animal attacks, and their bodies prepared to respond to the threat through a series of observable physiological changes, such as pupil dilation to improve vision and sharpening their hearing. In preparation for a challenge, the body used to tense the muscles and increased blood flow to the brain to support mental processes.

This resulted in an increase in heart and respiratory rate, while the limbs may have felt cold and sweaty. In today's world, we may not have to deal with wild animals, but we do have to deal with various situations such as work-related problems, marital problems, school-related stress, and so on. If our body fails to release itself from the changes that occur during the recognition phase of the threat, we may enter a state of chronic stress. When we are stressed and are exposed to additional stressors, the brain's regulating centers may overreact, causing physical wear and tear, emotional distress (such as crying spells), and in severe cases, depression and suicidal thoughts.

The third source of stress comes from our thoughts. The way we interpret our experiences and envision the future can either relax us or stress us out. Thinking about problems creates tension in the body, which in turn generates a feeling of unease, leading to more anxious thoughts.

Although everyone is susceptible to stress, some are more vulnerable than others. It is important to note that two people exposed to the same stressful event or circumstance may react differently. The interpretation of the event is often more significant than the event itself. The level of stress is determined by our perception of an event and our ability to cope with it. For instance, taking an exam is not in itself stressful; it is stressful for the student who has not studied enough, while for the one who has prepared well, the test will not be a stressful situation.

The mind and body are interconnected, and our physical state reflects our thoughts, emotions, and actions. Therefore, when we experience anxiety or anger, our body signals that something is wrong.

We cannot avoid all stressful situations in our lives or prevent the development of an innate response to the threats we face. However, we can learn to counteract our typical stress reactions by practicing relaxation techniques.

Psychologist Daniel Goleman[7] suggests that relaxation and meditation are closely linked to positive mental states. According to him, the mind can produce healing changes in the body. When a person realizes that their discomforts result from erroneous or unrealistic thoughts and expectations, they can think more rationally and experience better health.

People with good emotional health are aware of their thoughts, feelings, and actions. By using effective stress-coping mechanisms, individuals can improve their self-esteem and maintain healthy relationships. However, this requires following specific steps:

- Identify emotions and uncover the causes of stress, sadness, or anxiety.
- Express feelings appropriately. If feelings of sadness or anger are not expressed, it can lead to physical problems.
- Maintain a balanced life where work, home, school, family, and friendships all receive their deserved time and attention.
- Engage in activities that are enjoyable, because even in difficult times, positive engagement can improve quality of life and have a positive impact on health.
- Take care of the body by maintaining a regular routine of healthy eating, getting enough sleep, and exercising to relieve accumulated tension. Using drugs or alcohol brings about greater health problems and family issues.

The Social Readjustment Rating Scale[8]

The Social Readjustment Rating Scale, also known as the Holmes and Rahe Stress Scale, was developed in 1967 by psychiatrists Thomas Holmes and Richard Rahe to study the links between stress and illness.

They examined the medical records of more than 5,000 patients, and focused specifically on 43 common life events. Participants were asked to report which of these events, called Life Change Units (LCUs), they had experienced in the previous two years. This allowed Holmes and Rahe to determine the relative "weight" of different types of stress.

To score your stress levels, simply decide whether each of the events in the Statements column has happened to you in the last year, selecting Yes or No and add up the scores. If the total is below 150, the risk of falling ill due to stress is low. If the total falls between 151 and 299, the risk is moderate. Scores above 300 indicate a significant risk of falling ill due to stress.

43 Statements to Answer	Yes	No
Death of a spouse (100)		
Divorce (73)		
Marital separation (65)		
Jail term (63)		

43 Statements to Answer	**Yes**	**No**
Death of a close family member (63)		
Personal injury or illness (53)		
Marriage (50)		
Fired at work (47)		
Marital reconciliation (45)		
Retirement (45)		
Change in health of family member (44)		
Pregnancy (40)		
Sex difficulties (39)		
Gain of new family member (39)		
Business readjustment (39)		
Change in financial state (38)		
Death of a close friend (37)		

43 Statements to Answer	Yes	No
Change to a different line of work (36)		
Change in number of arguments with spouse (35)		
A large mortgage or loan (31)		
Foreclosure of mortgage or loan (30)		
Change in responsibilities at work (29)		
Son or daughter leaving home (29)		
Trouble with in-laws (29)		
Outstanding personal achievement (28)		
Spouse begins or stops work (26)		
Begin or end school/college (26)		
Change in living conditions (25)		
Revision of personal habits (24)		
Trouble with boss (23)		

43 Statements to Answer	Yes	No
Change in work hours or conditions (20)		
Change in residence (20)		
Change in school/college (20)		
Change in recreation (19)		
Change in church activities (19)		
Change in social activities (18)		
A moderate loan or mortgage (17)		
Change in sleeping habits (16)		
Change in number of family get-togethers (15)		
Change in eating habits (15)		
Vacation (13)		
Christmas (12)		
Minor violations of the law (11)		

5

DONT LET ANGER TAKE OVER

William Foster is a regular citizen who is on his way to his daughter's house to celebrate her birthday, despite his ex-wife's request that he not attend.

On the hottest day of the year, Foster finds himself trapped in the intense traffic of Los Angeles. He abandons his car and continues on foot, dressed impeccably in a white shirt and dark tie. His journey takes him to a grocery store where he confronts the abusive prices of products, encounters some street thugs, interacts with employees at a fast-food restaurant, and even crosses paths with a neo-Nazi.

Due to his frustrations, Foster rebels in a violent and destructive way against everything around him. A police officer is the only one who tries to stop his violent and aggressive behavior.

We have all experienced anger at some point, which is a normal emotion. However, when it is out of control, it can become a destructive force that leads to negative consequences.

Falling Down[9], a 1990s film starring Michael Douglas, features William Foster as a character showing how unhealthy emotions can manifest violently, like an exploding pressure cooker.

It is common and healthy to feel angry from time to time in response to certain situations. However, sometimes people experience uncontrollable anger that often escalates into a major problem.

Over 2,000 years ago, Aristotle, the Greek philosopher, stated in his classic work 'Poetics' that watching tragic theatrical performances can offer the possibility of catharsis[10]. This is a psychological purification that allows one to release anger and negative emotions.

Sigmund Freud, the Austrian psychoanalyst, believed that repressed anger could escalate and worsen to the point of causing psychological illnesses such as hysteria. He proposed the use of catharsis[11] as a way of talking about negative feelings to release them in a controlled manner.

For instance, consider the movie *Analyze This*[12], where a psychiatrist advises a New York gangster, played by Robert de Niro, to hit a pillow whenever he gets angry. In *Anger Management*[13], Adam Sandler is unfairly accused of having "anger issues" on a flight, and the judge orders him to attend an anger management group where he has to throw golf clubs to release his anger.

Similarly, it is often suggested that instead of suppressing negative emotions, we should punch a pillow or sandbag hard while yelling. If we are angry with someone in particular, we should imagine their face on the pillow or sandbag and express the anger physically and verbally.

Could William Foster, the protagonist of *Falling Down*, have released his pent-up emotions by hitting one of the seats with his fist to vent his anger? Some research[14] suggests that the hypothesis of catharsis expressed in physical acts is false; the expression of anger, either directly at a person or indirectly at an object, actually leads to more aggression.

It is important to note that physical action is not an effective way to release anger. Studying the following techniques can help people better understand how to deal with their anger. The three main approaches are expressing, suppressing and calming.

Expressing

Expressing angry feelings assertively, not aggressively, is the healthiest way to communicate anger. To achieve this, you must learn to clearly express your needs and how to meet them without causing harm to others. Being assertive does not mean being pushy or demanding, but rather to be respectful of yourself and others. For example, consider a scenario where your neighbor consistently parks his car in front of your driveway: If this situation upsets you, yelling at them or damaging their car will not make you feel better; instead, expressing your annoyance firmly may help resolve the conflict. In this case, expressing feelings of anger in an assertive, non-aggressive way can be a healthy way to deal with anger, such as saying something like "I understand that you don't mean to do this, but it really bothers me when you park your car in front of my driveway because I can't get in".

Suppressing

Suppressing anger and redirecting it can be a useful technique. This can be done by holding in your anger, stopping yourself from thinking about it and focusing on something positive. The aim is to inhibit or suppress your anger and convert it into constructive behavior. However, it is important to note that suppressing anger can also have negative consequences if not done properly. If outward expression of anger is not allowed, it can turn inward and cause harm to oneself. Exercise can be effective in managing anger, while writing about the thoughts and feelings associated with the event can help transform the initial emotion into something more objective and constructive. Focusing on alternative activities rather than the situation that caused the anger can help us analyze and understand it from another perspective.

Calming

Calming yourself down inside means not just controlling your outward behavior but also controlling your internal responses, taking steps to lower your heart rate, calming yourself down and taking the time to allow the immediate feelings to subside. You can use techniques like listening to relaxing music, meditation, and intentional deep breathing to manage negative emotions.

What do you think of these techniques? Are you ready to try some of these different ways of dealing with your negative emotions?

6

ARE YOU A "WORKAHOLIC"?

When you leave work before your colleagues, do you feel like you are acting wrong? Do you receive phone calls from your workplace requiring more of your attention even after you return home? Does your job take priority over everything else, including your family? Do you frequently bring home extra work to finish during evenings or weekends? Be careful! Enjoying your work and being committed to the company are positive qualities, but being addicted or enslaved to your work is quite different.

Some people are so devoted to their work that they become absorbed in it, to the point where it seems they live only to work. This is known as work addiction.

People who suffer from work addiction believe that the more time they spend at the office, the more efficient they are, and in extreme cases, they only come home to sleep, completely abandoning their personal and social lives. Moreover, for some, work is the perfect refuge to avoid facing everyday situations or to forget about family problems.

The term *workaholic* refers to an employee who enjoys his work, loves it, but has become addicted to it; in short, he is someone who lives for his work and demands much more of himself than the company requires of him. This type of worker has always existed, but the term became more popular in the 1980s when the effects of excessive work on personal life and health began to be described, in addition to being associated with certain forms of stress and personality disorders. For example, obsessive-compulsive personality disorder[15] is characterized by excessive dedication to work and productivity, often at the expense of leisure and socializing. In general, this behavior is not motivated by economic needs, so people do not necessarily work to earn more money, but because working is satisfying to them. In addition, many of these individuals have low self-esteem and associate their personal worth with their professional success.

Workaholics often believe that they do not have time to take an afternoon off, a weekend off, or simply to relax, and they postpone pleasurable activities (like taking a vacation) indefinitely.

If a workaholic does engage in leisure activities, they may feel uncomfortable unless they bring along some work tasks. This allows them to stop feeling guilty about 'wasting' time.

Another characteristic of workaholics is that they treat hobbies or recreational activities as serious tasks that require careful organization and hard work to perform well. For example, when playing a tennis match or a board game, they put in the same effort as when organizing a work meeting.

Work addiction affects both men and women, and it is estimated that over 20% of the global working population experiences this addiction.

In Japan, a country that is known for its high level of development, the culture of work is deeply rooted. The term *karoshi*[16] was coined to describe a social phenomenon that has existed for several decades in the country's work environment. It refers to an increase in the mortality rate due to complications caused by excessive work activity, especially as a result of strokes and heart attacks preceded by prolonged periods of stress and tension.

According to data from the International Labour Organization (ILO),[17] 36% of the world's workers work more than 48 hours per week, and work-related illnesses cause 2.4 million deaths annually. Other physical consequences of work addiction may include fatigue, chronic tiredness, irritability, anxiety attacks, headaches, neck and back pain, gastritis, irritable bowel syndrome, hypertension, and cardiovascular problems. Furthermore, work addiction can lead to a state of deep depression.

In conclusion, work has become a source of stress and dissatisfaction for many people, despite its purpose of providing economic, psychological, and social rewards and giving meaning to our lives. Therefore, it is important to take a moment to reflect on our priorities in life, analyzing whether they truly deserve our attention, and ultimately, making changes for the benefit of our physical and mental health.

How to break work addiction

These are the guidelines you can follow to achieve a balance between your professional and personal life:

- Gradually reduce work hours.
- Set a consistent work schedule. Take into account rest periods and time off.
- Do not take work home.
- Learn how to prioritize activities.
- Learn how to delegate tasks to your colleagues.
- Schedule time to spend with your spouse, kids, and friends.
- Strengthen personal and family relationships to spend more time with those you care about.

WHAT IS THE PURPOSE OF MY LIFE?

While looking in the mirror and realizing that you are getting older, or realizing that you never got that job you wanted or the health you wished for, have you ever asked yourself what the meaning of your life is? Why are you here? If you are unable to answer these questions, if you feel empty or incomplete but don't know why, if you are living in search of something without knowing what you hope to find, and if you consider your life to be an accident, let me tell you the story of a man who found the answer to these questions.

Viktor Frankl was a Viennese physician of Jewish origin who was deported to various concentration camps for three years during World War II. Despite holding a visa to immigrate to the United States in search of a promising future, he chose to remain in Vienna with his parents and his young wife, Tilly. However, in the fall of 1942, he was taken, along with his entire family, to a concentration camp.

Frankl survived the Jewish extermination by working twelve hours a day, often in the snow, sometimes having only a ration of soup and a piece of bread as his sole food. On many occasions, he felt the urge to throw himself against the electrified fences to end his suffering, as many prisoners did. However, the memory of his wife and his desire to see her again kept him alive.

At the end of the war, he was forced to confront the harsh reality of the situation: his parents, his brother, and even his wife, who had been his reason for living during his imprisonment, had died in the concentration camps or had been sent to the gas chambers. As a result, with the exception of his sister Stella, who had managed to emigrate to Australia shortly before, Frankl found himself completely alone.

Perhaps you wonder how a man who lost practically everything worthwhile in his life, who experienced the brutalities of war, hunger, and cold, who was on the verge of death several times, could consider that life was still worth living.

Viktor Frankl recognized that even in the most challenging circumstances, where dehumanization and suffering are extreme, a person can find reasons to live. He found a new purpose in life by developing logotherapy (a therapy that helps people find their life's meaning) and by sharing his experiences in the book *Man's Search for Meaning*[18], which is one of the most influential literary works of recent times.

The life of Viktor Frankl demonstrates that even in the most challenging circumstances, human beings can survive by discovering the purpose of their existence.

The meaning of life is the reason we exist. In essence, it is the answer to the question: What is the purpose of my existence? Answering this question is not simple, as the purpose of life is different for each person, and it is built and also evolves, day by day.

The meaning of life is not a destination to be reached, but

rather a personal journey to be traveled.

The meaning of life is the specific significance that each individual assigns to their journey. Each person has a specific purpose or mission to fulfill. What is important to one individual may not be meaningful to another, and what is meaningful to the latter may lack value to the former. In the absence of a clear purpose in life, many people prioritize accumulating wealth or collecting romantic relationships. The unemployed experience depression, and even the wealthy are unhappy. Each of us must find the meaning that allows us to make the most of our journey through this world.

According to Frankl, there are three ways we can find meaning in our lives:

1) Having a cause to serve. When we apply our skills and talents to serve others and promote social improvement, we gain a sense of purpose and direction in life. We understand that a meaningful life is one that is spent serving others and contributing to a larger, more meaningful cause.

2) Having someone with whom to love.

3) Finding Meaning in Suffering: Does suffering offer a way to find meaning in life? Yes. Consider, for example, a person facing a terminal illness. Their situation, which is very painful, can be mitigated if they decide to participate in an organ donation program. A great example of how we can find meaning in suffering is the story of Ismael Khatib, a Palestinian refugee whose eleven-year-old son, Ahmed, was shot by Israeli soldiers. Instead of seeking revenge, this father donated his son's organs to Israeli children.[19] His decision (with the consent of his wife) demonstrates humanity in the moment of greatest sorrow. Instead of dwelling on their suffering, these parents focused their attention on the positive impact they will have on others through their organ donation.

In such circumstances, humans are able to accept suffering if it has a purpose, as Frankl demonstrated after the loss of his loved ones. His suffering was expressed through his theoretical creativity and the foundation of logotherapy.

When seeking the meaning of our lives, we must be aware that perhaps the most important thing is to understand what life expects from us, rather than what we expect from life.

If you're unsure of how to begin identifying your purpose, consider the following questions as a starting point: When in your life have you felt proud or satisfied with something you did? Which activities do you enjoy intensely that make you feel fulfilled? What matters most to you in life? How would you like to be remembered when you die?

How different our lives become when we realize that we don't just live for the sake of living, but we have a responsibility in this world that compels us to continue until we fulfill our mission. How many people spend their lives "searching for something" without knowing what it is, and don't see it even when they find it! How many people are simply born... and die without fulfilling a mission!

**"Man does not simply exist,
but always decides what his existence will be,
what he will become in the next moment."[20]**

Viktor Frankl

In conclusion, we have the option of pursuing a life without meaning, where our actions lack significance and from which we derive no satisfaction. Or we may choose to focus on a life plan where our activities and projects allow us to realize our capacity to create our reality.

We have the freedom to make our own choices. Viktor Frankl was not able to choose whether he would be imprisoned in a concentration camp. However, he was able to choose how he would behave during his captivity.

In any situation, it is the responsibility of each individual to take control of their own destiny and become an active participant in their own life, rather than merely observing it "from the outside". We are the architects of our own destinies. Therefore, it is our responsibility to fully embrace the opportunity we have been given so that at the end of our lives, we can be grateful for having lived rather than regretting merely having existed.

"Everything can be taken from a man but one thing: the last of the human freedoms to choose one's attitude in any given set of circumstances, to choose one's own way."[21]

Viktor Frankl

8

THE MULTI-PROBLEM FAMILY

Jeanette is a successful journalist in New York, about to get married and seemingly living a happy life. One night, after leaving a party, she finds her parents scavenging for food in the garbage, and her seemingly perfect life begins to crumble. In reality, Jeanette and her three siblings had grown up in a nomadic and dysfunctional family, living in abandoned houses to avoid paying rent. Constantly moving from place to place to avoid creditors and authorities, the children did not attend school and sometimes went without food. The four siblings had learned to take care of themselves because their parents didn't act like parents: their father, an intelligent and creative man, was an irresponsible alcoholic, dissatisfied with the system, who distracted his children with the constant promise of building a glass castle. Their mother, on the other hand, was a frustrated painter who avoided the responsibility of raising her children. With much effort and in secret from their parents, the siblings one day managed to escape the nightmare their family had become and moved to New York.

The true story of Jeannette Walls, brought to the screen in the movie "The Glass Castle"[22] is a perfect example of a family in which disorganization and a lack of defined roles led to conflict. Jeannette, played by Brie Larson, and her siblings witness their parents (Woody Harrelson and Naomi Watts) fighting and become victims of their misguided arguments.

Under the pretext of freedom and the desire to live without constraints, these parents let their children grow up adrift and without stability, while they themselves remain irresponsible, careless, and selfish.

Problematic families,[23] like the one mentioned above, are characterized mainly by disorganization, problems in the development and establishment of roles, especially parental roles (the functions performed by each family member are not clearly defined), and inadequate attention to economic matters and the care of children. Unimportant activities take precedence over others, and little value is placed on communication and the establishment of basic rules.

It is also common in these families for one or both partners to have a history of school maladjustment, addiction, or other problematic behaviors. Parents often have a conflicted relationship and fail to provide their children with a deep sense of being loved and valued, often even abusing them. This situation also means that there are no consistent rules of behavior for children to learn from, leading them to associate prohibitions and punishments with the moods of the parent in power. In addition, families with limited resources, like the one depicted in "The Glass Castle," have fewer cultural and educational opportunities. Often, school is seen as unimportant compared to getting a job, even though education is essential for future success.

Another common characteristic of this type of family is the lack of defined spaces: children, adolescents, and adults may not have their own rooms or personal spaces. The consequence of sharing spaces is that roles and relationships among family members are not clearly defined.

Thus, depending on how they are structured, we can find different examples of problematic families.

Families with poorly defined roles

There are families in which the roles of parents and children are so poorly defined that it sometimes seems that the children, rather than the parents, are in charge of the household. This loss of roles occurs because parents are unable to discipline, do not want to be authoritarian, and do not dare to say anything that might contradict their children's wishes, without upsetting them. Since everything is allowed in this type of family, the children end up doing what they want without any form of structure or direction.

Overprotective families

There are also families that are overly protective of their children, preventing them from developing autonomy and personal identity. Such parents believe that without their help and care, the children will not be able to fend for themselves, face the world, or earn a living. By overprotecting them, they delay their maturation process. The result is that they create unnecessarily dependent and insecure children.

Families resistant to change

Another type of family style is characterized by parents who have difficulty accepting the changes their children are going through. Even though time passes and their children are no longer children, they continue to treat them as if they were. By not accepting that their children have grown up, they become rigid and intolerant toward them. For example, during adolescence, when a child asks for permission to go to a party or to sleep over at his best friend's house, he may receive an automatic "no" without any explanation other than authoritarian phrases like "because I said so" or "because you live in my house".

Child-Centered Families

On the other hand, we also find families where the parents center their lives around their children. This means that the children are the focal point and all attention is given to them, so much so that the couple never discusses their own affairs. Not knowing how to face their own conflicts and marital dissatisfaction, parents use their children as the only topic of conversation, seek them out for companionship, and live exclusively for them, since their personal satisfaction depends on them.

As we can see, the common thread of unstable or troubled families is disunity. The parents, who are the heads of the family, lack common goals, principles, or values to instill in their children. Unconsciously encouraged are behaviors of instability, insecurity, mistrust, and an inability to communicate feelings.

It has been found that living in a family emotional climate characterized by conflict and constant friction can have very negative health consequences. According to several studies,[24] problematic relationships with parents, siblings, or close family members can contribute to the development or worsening of chronic conditions such as stroke and headaches.

Therefore, if we want to promote harmonious family relationships rich with by communication, trust, support and unity among all its members, we begin by establishing clear and defined roles, values and disciplinary rules.

Let us not forget that the family is the fundamental structure of society, the point of reference in the life of each person, where the first emotional bonds are formed and where our personality, values and behavioral patterns are formed and developed.

**Members of united families are more secure,
stable, and self-confident.
They grow up with clear goals
and become independent, healthy adults.**

PUT YOURSELF IN SOMEONE ELSE'S SHOES

Let's consider a married couple seeking psychotherapy due to the husband's lack of sensitivity to feelings, despite his professional success and intelligence as a doctor. He has excellent communication skills, particularly in the medical field. However, he lacks the ability to express his emotions or understand those of his wife. If she expresses sadness, he fails to comprehend her feelings, chooses to ignore her, or changes the subject.

The previous example is a clear case of a lack of empathy. Empathy is the ability to put oneself in another's place, to respond with an appropriate feeling to another person's perspective or emotions, to understand how and why the other person feels that way, and to do so from the perspective of another person's beliefs and values, not from one's own perspective.

The term "empathy," which we colloquially refer to as "putting yourself in someone else's shoes," was coined in the 1920s by the American psychologist Edward B. Titchener when referring to the ability to perceive another person's subjective experience.

Empathy is developed when individuals are aware of their own emotions and are able to interpret both their own feelings and those of others. When an individual lacks awareness of their own emotions, they may struggle to empathize with the feelings of others. The tone of voice, change in posture, an awkward silence or even visible trembling may be overlooked. Similarly, an individual lacking empathy may experience confusion when another person expresses their feelings of neglect.

The social skill of understanding another person's emotions is applicable to a multitude of scenarios, including parenting, professional work, social responsibility, and political activity.

The lack of empathy is a significant issue. It is present in all types of criminals and psychopaths. What are the origins of empathy? Is empathy an innate capacity, or can it be learned?

According to Titchener[25], empathy is triggered by a physical imitation of another individual's emotional distress, which evokes a corresponding emotional response in the other person. The American psychologist references a case study of a nursery baby who injured his fingers while playing and started crying. Another baby imitated the injured baby to determine whether the same result would occur in him.

Research indicates that babies demonstrate genuine concern for others, even before they fully understand that they are separate beings from their mothers.[26] Shortly after birth, for example, babies can react to the distress of those around them as if it were their own, and they cry when they see another child's tears. At around one year of age, children begin to understand that the distress of another is not their own, yet they remain confused and unsure of how to respond.

When does empathy begin to develop?

It is only when a child has developed a sense of self as distinct from others that they are able to appropriately respond to the emotions and feelings of others. At approximately two years of age, children frequently experience distress when observing another child suffering and approach them to offer a toy or provide a hug.[27]

Have you ever observed a child expressing distress when they observe another child being hurt and then seeking comfort from their own mother, as if they themselves were the victim? This act of solidarity demonstrates that the roots of empathy are developed in childhood.

One of the most famous phrases in literature, attributed to the English poet John Donne, says: "No man is an island. Any man's death diminishes me, because I am involved in mankind. And therefore, never send to know for whom the bell tolls; it tolls for thee.,"[28] and it serves to express the connection between empathy and concern: feeling the pain of others as if it were one's own.

Caring for others is an act of empathy. It involves re cognizing another's distress and acting to support them.

This was evident in the cases of the cited babies, where empathy motivated them to act in order to help or support.

Empathy has a number of positive aspects, including facilitating communication, providing comfort, and enabling problem-solving. Empathy is demonstrated when we are able to listen and understand another person's feelings without being overly focused on ourselves. We are able to offer a pat on the shoulder, a hug, a caress, or a kiss in addition to words of consolation. In contrast, when we fail to listen to others' opinions, when we believe our problems are the only ones that matter, when we make negative comments or when we fail to offer a smile, a kind gesture, or a touch to others, we are demonstrating a lack of empathy.

How can we develop empathy?

- Demonstrating respect for others and refraining from judgment.
- Listening attentively and demonstrating interest in what others are saying.
- Demonstrating to the other person that we understand how they feel.
- Do not interrupt while the other person is speaking.
- Avoid making comments and instead attempt to empathize with the other person's feelings.
- Providing constructive feedback without causing any harm to the person receiving it.
- Being tolerant and patient with others.

And so we've learned that, it is always desirable to put ourselves in the "shoes of others," but we must be careful not to absorb emotions. This means that we should not take the feelings of the other person as our own, as this can result in an emotional disconnection from ourselves and this might happen a high cost. We must first take care of ourselves.

We'll summarize with a memorable anecdote to bring the point home. When sitting with seatbelt fastened as the plane is about to take off from the airport, the flight attendant always makes sure to repeat the same instructions no matter who the passengers are, no matter which airline or in which country, the instructions are always the same, "Ladies and gentlemen, in case of an emergency, an oxygen mask will drop down from the compartment above you. Please make sure to put the mask on yourself before attempting to help others.

10

"MOM, I DON'T WANT TO GO
TO CLASS ANYMORE!"

Alejandra is a 17-year-old teenager who loses her mother in a car accident. She then moves with her father to another city, hoping to start a new life in a place that doesn't bring back sad memories. She begins to socialize successfully with her new classmates until a sexual encounter with one of them is recorded by a cell phone. At that point, she becomes the victim of bullying and harassment. She remains silent out of concern for her father, who is still grieving the loss of his wife. She endures a significant amount of aggression until the day she breaks down and runs away from everything.

The above is a synopsis of the Mexican film *After Lucia*,[29] in which the protagonist finds herself in a position of helplessness against the world, and her tormentors take every opportunity to turn her existence into life into a nightmare.

Many of us have the naive impression that bullying at school consists of innocent teasing, throwing paper balls, or giving out nicknames. In general, we are not prepared for the level of bullying depicted in *After Lucia*.

The term "bullying" was developed in the 1970s and comes from the word "bully," which means someone who hurts or frightens someone else. In this sense, bullying, or

61

school harassment, refers to behaviors that repeatedly and over time involve intimidation, threats, social isolation, and insults directed at a victim. It can also include hitting or kicking other classmates, taunting, giving nicknames, hiding backpacks, manipulating, forcing others to do things against their will, etc. However, the most important aspect is not the act itself, but the effect it has on the victim.

If you've noticed that your child comes home from school sad, downcast, missing some of his or her belongings, or even injured, don't make light of the situation. They may be the victim of bullying, which, in addition to causing poor academic performance, can permanently damage their self-esteem and affect them for life.

Bullying is not new, as school violence has always existed; however, its effects are more visible now because it affects more people and the media has a greater power of dissemination.

There are different types of school bullying, and one can be a victim of several at the same time.

Physical Bullying

This is defined as any form of physical intimidation or harassment directed towards a student, including but not limited to pushing, kicking, or being attacked with objects. It also includes the theft of personal belongings such as backpacks, lunches, or sweaters.

Verbal Bullying

Verbal bullying is the most common form of bullying,

where students are subjected to insults, teasing, and derogatory nicknames that target their physical characteristics as flaws. For instance, a student wearing glasses might be called "Four Eyes," and a student who is overweight might be called "Fatty."

Social bullying

Social bullying is defined as the deliberate exclusion of a student from their classmates by prohibiting them from playing or socializing with a group, from talking or communicating with others, or simply by treating them as if they didn't exist.

Psychological bullying

Psychological bullying has a diminishing effect on an individual's self-esteem and increases their sense of fear through words, looks, or insinuations that destabilize them until the child loses confidence in themselves. This can be exemplified by a teacher criticizing students who don't answer questions or shouting at children who get up from their seats.

Cyberbullying

Cyberbullying is one of the most prevalent forms of harassment in the modern era. Such cyberbullying is carried out through a variety of digital channels, including cell phones, the internet, emails, and social media. The objective of the bully is to damage the victim's reputation by posting false information, spying on them, or manipulating others to turn against them.

As can be seen, in every instance of bullying, at least two

individuals are involved: the perpetrator and the victim. However, the specific roles each individual plays are not merely accidental.

In general, the aggressor is impulsive and physically stronger, may be popular and outgoing, and may also be boastful. In some cases, they are fully aware that their actions are causing harm. In other instances, however, they may simply believe that what they are doing is enjoyable.

In contrast, the victim is typically insecure, introverted, and shy, with low self-esteem and a high level of anxiety, making them susceptible to bullying. They may appear to be dependent and attached to home, or conversely, they may lack affection. In addition, they frequently have difficulty making friends.

The victim's physical appearance also sets them apart, as they may be noticed for their physical traits such as wearing glasses, being overweight, or their skin or hair color. They may also stand out due being identified by a minority group, such as being a female in a group predominantly composed of males.

A third party also plays a role in *bullying*, even if they are not directly involved. This is the bystander, or the individual who witnesses the bullying. Often, they find amusement in the situation and take the side of the aggressor because it makes them feel powerful. Alternatively, they may choose not to intervene or speak out due to fear of becoming victims themselves. Bystanders play a crucial role in either perpetuating or mitigating bullying situations.

It is evident that the individual most adversely affected

by bullying is the victim, who experiences the most significant consequences. The academic performance of these students declines, they exhibit high levels of anxiety, and in some cases, they develop a fear of school. Such victims frequently experience low self-esteem, depressive episodes, and in more severe cases, may even attempt suicide.

The World Health Organization (WHO) has identified bullying as the leading cause of adolescent suicide. UNICEF data[30] indicates that approximately half of the world's adolescents experience violence in schools, with an estimated 150 million students aged 13 to 15 years reporting some form of violence among their peers at school.

To prevent extreme situations, it is crucial for parents and teachers—who are often the last to be aware of what is happening to children—to be able to identify which student is experiencing school bullying. The following are some indications that may be helpful in identifying students who are experiencing school bullying:

- Changes in the behavior and mood of the child.
- Sadness, crying, or irritability.
- Changes in sleep and/or appetite.
- Frequent loss or damage to belongings (glasses, backpack, pencil case, torn pants, etc.).
- Presence of bruises or scratches (the child often claims to have falls or accidents).
- Lack of interaction with classmates.
- Wanting to be accompanied to school entry and exit.
- Refusing to go to classes or protesting about it.
- Not participating in school outings, visits, or trips.

Once these behaviors have been identified, it is crucial for parents to establish a close relationship with their child's teacher, get to know their classmates, and identify their friends to gain a comprehensive understanding of their relationships. It is important to maintain consistent communication with the child and to dispel the misconception that the issue will resolve itself with age or by moving to the next school year.

The long-term effects of *bullying* can have a significant impact on an individual's life. It is, therefore, essential to seek help as soon as possible.

It is important to have the support of a psychologist or specialist in school bullying, family support, and a group of close friends to help with recovery and return to normal life as soon as possible.

11

IS YOUR RELATIONSHIP A LIVING HELL?

As a child, Leticia - now 54 years old - witnessed the scene of her alcoholic father murdering her mother in a fit of jealousy. She was then taken to live with her maternal grandmother, who, instead of providing her with love and care, treated her like a domestic servant. Tired of the abuse, at the age of 16 Leticia abandoned her grandmother and, having nowhere else to go, spent her first night on the streets, where a group of vandals sexually abused her. After that, Leticia wandered from place to place looking for shelter and food, until an elderly woman took her into her home in exchange for help with household chores. Soon after, she met Saul, a man who was kind and attentive to her, and whom she soon married. However, it was not long before her husband began to insult her and beat her, because, according to him, Leticia was a " solicitor" with all men. After that, the beatings came for no reason, especially when Saul got drunk. For many years, Leticia thought that the way her husband treated her was normal because it was the same treatment she had received as a child. She even believed that Saul loved her and was sure that he would change, thinking that deep down he wasn't a bad person because he treated

67

her kindly when he wasn't drunk or angry. Recently, Leticia left the hospital where she spent the last week recovering from a beating Saul gave her; she nearly lost her left eye, but "luckily" suffered only a few fractures. She returned home with a cast on her arm and a neck brace. When I last saw her, Leticia had begun psychotherapy, as recommended by the authorities to whom she had legally reported her husband.

**Domestic violence is the abuse that typically occurs
between members of a couple, as they are the ones
who directly experience the aggression. However,
its effects extend to the entire family, including children,
who witness the ever-present conflict between their parents.**

According to the World Health Organization (WHO),[31] violence against women is a global health problem of epidemic proportions, affecting more than one-third of all women worldwide. The WHO estimates that approximately 35% of women will experience violence at some point in their lives, either from their partner or from someone outside the relationship. In addition, 38% of women are murdered at the hands of their partners.

Domestic violence is a significant trigger for women's mental health problems. Research has shown that women who have experienced partner violence are almost twice as likely to suffer from depression as those who have not. In addition, it has been found that women who suffer from partner violence are almost twice as likely to have problems with alcohol abuse compared to non-victims.

Various studies reveal that experiencing violence during childhood is often a significant factor in perpetuating it into adolescence and adulthood. In addition, households where women are abused by their partners tend to have more cases of child abuse than households without domestic violence. In addition, a woman's likelihood of experiencing partner violence is associated with a history of intrafamilial violence during childhood.

The cycle of violence[32] is a process by which violence in a couple's relationship unfolds. It is characterized by periods of calm and stability interspersed with disagreements, arguments, and tension. These conflicts can escalate until they culminate in physical aggression. Following the violence, there is a phase of calm and "reconciliation," during which the aggressor (typically the man) apologizes to the victim, expresses remorse, and promises to change. While there may be a period of improvement in the relationship, old patterns of relating tend to reemerge, leading to friction and arguments once again. This can eventually result in another violent episode, followed by another reconciliation. This process can continue indefinitely.

In a couple's relationship, it is crucial to maintain a balance of love, respect, admiration, and companionship. When these values are absent, the relationship is at risk of failure, and in many cases, abuse, harm, and offensive behaviors emerge.

Causes

Why do women tend to tolerate mistreatment from their men, whether psychological, physical, or both? Is it possible for an abused woman to love her abuser? What factors contribute to an abused woman remaining in the relationship despite the abuse? Why does she not leave him?

To address these questions, we will refer to the case of Leticia, who claimed to be in love with Saul because, when she met him, he was the only person who had treated her well in her life. She was so absorbed in the ideal image she had created of him that she failed to recognize the reality of the situation, which led her to endure all kinds of abuse. Despite his mistreatment of his wife, Saul was generous when he was not in a rage and could be reasonably affectionate, which helped fulfill the affectionate void Leticia had experienced throughout her life.

Due to her low self-esteem, there were times when Leticia felt that Saul's aggressions were justified, and she tried to convince herself that her husband would change at some point in the future. The first time she attempted to leave him, Saul threatened to harm her or take away her children. At the same time, he emphasized that Leticia would be unable to support herself financially without his assistance, given her lack of skilled employment.

One of the main reasons Leticia remained in the abusive relationship with Saul was due to a sense of shame. She was reluctant to acknowledge the abuse, which led to her maintaining secrecy. Additionally, Leticia endured her husband for an extended period of time, hoping he would change. As a result, she began to accept the violence as a normal aspect of their relationship.

How domestic violence should be handled?

Domestic violence is not just a matter of physical injuries. It is a social issue that affects women of all ages and social classes. Individuals and governmental institutions become accomplices when they remain silent and fail to act.

The case of Ana Orantes,[33] who was murdered in 1997 by her ex-husband after publicly exposing the violence she endured throughout their 40 years of marriage, on a television program, is an example. It was widely documented by the Spanish press. Prior to finally obtaining a divorce, Ana had reported her partner's assaults on multiple occasions. However, she received only the response from the authorities that the incidents were "normal family disputes".

The first step in dealing with domestic violence is to eliminate beliefs that condone its use against any family member as a way to resolve differences. Some justify the use of physical force as a means of conflict resolution, but fail to recognize that subsequent actions could have more severe consequences.

800,000 women die each year worldwide as a result of any type of violence.

Once a person is involved in a situation of violence, his or her family and friends must act as a support network. It is crucial to seek professional help, submit the necessary reports, and participate in psychological therapy to improve self-esteem and regain a sense of dignity and self-respect. Never forget that one of the main characteristics of violent relationships is the devaluation and undermining of self-esteem.

We cannot over emphasize that no one comes out of a situation of violence unharmed. If we do not stop it, we run the risk that those who have suffered violence will go through life reproducing or normalizing the same violence, seeing it as something to be expected, as something that just "happens". On the contrary, if we see violence as something avoidable, reprehensible, and problematic, we can take steps to avoid it and to change ourselves and our environment.

12

WHAT DO DREAMS MEAN?

The interpretation of dreams has been a subject of study since ancient times. In classical Greece, dreams were considered supernatural experiences, sources of divination to predict future events, and a way to communicate with the gods. Aristotle (384-322 B.C.) viewed dreams as a distinct form of waking experience that reflected the emotional needs of the waking person. In addition, many cultures attribute prophetic value to dreams, as in the Bible, where Joseph interprets Pharaoh's dreams, through which he prevents starvation from an imminent famine in Egypt.

The most famous theory of dream interpretation was proposed by the Austrian physician Sigmund Freud, the founder of psychoanalysis, in his book "*The Interpretation of Dreams*,"[34] published in 1899. Freud used his own dreams to demonstrate his theory on the psychology of dreams, suggesting that they clearly reveal unconscious mental processes.

From a psychoanalytic perspective, we all have a conscious and a subconscious part of our mind. When we wake up, what we can remember from our dream belongs to the conscious part. What we cannot remember is stored in our unconscious mind. Dreams therefore serve as a means of communication between the unconscious and the conscious mind; that's how unconscious content becomes conscious.

When the desires that a person experiences cannot be fulfilled because of social norms or repression, they are expressed through disguises and symbols in dreams. This was the theory of one of the great dream researchers, the psychoanalyst Sigmund Freud. Was he right?

Contrary to popular belief, we have dreams every night, although we often don't remember them and believe we haven't dreamed. While we sleep, our mind remains active, reviewing the events of the day, mixing them with memories from the past, and even creating new images. During sleep, many sensory stimuli continue to operate; some have the ability to wake us up, while others do not disturb our sleep.

For instance, the sound of a dripping faucet or the ticking of a wall clock can influence the content of our dreams. However, more often than not, the content of our dreams is related to thoughts and ideas that are connected to our daily activities and concerns. For instance, family or work-related issues frequently appear in dreams.

As Freud observed, humans are driven by a fundamental desire to obtain pleasure and avoid pain. However, in practice, it is not always possible to fulfill all our desires because we are constrained by social norms and repression. Dreams thus become one of the primary avenues for satisfying our desires and accessing realities that are beyond the reach of logic.

It is rarely the case that dreams make sense when we remember them. They often contain elements that seem strange, terrifying, or unsettling. Why do they seem so odd? During the night, our minds relax, and dreams feature figures, characters, places, fantastical beings, or monsters that "disguise" the true content of the dream. It is possible to encounter in the same dream places and people that have no relation to each other, or who lived in different times. It is therefore possible to have a dream where both your late grandfather, who passed away shortly after you were born, and your childhood best friend, whom you have not seen in many years, appear together. Such things are possible because dreams satisfy the most hidden desires, but through a disguise that hides a deeper truth, of which the dreamer does not want to become conscious. From a psychoanalytic perspective, a series of nonsensical dream images, when analyzed and interpreted by an expert, can be translated into a coherent set of sometimes related ideas.

To better understand this, let's consider the film "Spellbound"[35] directed by Alfred Hitchcock. In the film, a psychoanalyst contacts a patient who has amnesia but fears he may be a murderer. The doctor, played by Ingrid Bergman, evaluates and analyzes the patient's dreams, portrayed by Gregory Peck, to determine the source of his amnesia and whether it is due to guilt over committing a murder. In the patient's dreams, which feature surrealistic images lacking coherence (designed by Salvador Dalí), one can observe a number of unusual elements. These include enormous eyes on the walls, a man with giant scissors, a slanted roof, face-less men, broken wheels, a gambling house, and a chimney hiding a faceless man. After a thorough analysis of the dream, each seemingly disconnected element is revealed to have a clear significance. This allows the suspect to recall the events of the night and identify the true murderer.

Other perspectives that differ from psychoanalysis offer alternative insights. A number of studies have concluded that dreams are not the result of mental activity, but rather physiological processes. Dreams are explained as an unin-tended consequence of the REM phase of sleep, during which the eyes move rapidly. This phase is characterized by a state of relaxation and relative ease of awakening. During sleep, the brain receives significantly fewer muscle signals, allowing it to process and store memories.

Deirdre Barrett,[36] a Harvard University psychologist who has conducted numerous studies on dreams and has made significant contributions to the understanding of cre-ativity and problem solving, says that dreaming is like thinking when we are awake, but with different nuances, so that it is possible to solve problems while we are asleep. As examples, she cites prominent artists and scientists who have been inspired by their dreams.

Barrett suggests that dreams have evolved with humans, refining their essential functions, including helping the brain to "reset". She criticizes Freud's explanations of his time because the Austrian physician did not consider hu-man evolution and interpreted dreams as wish fulfillment in an imaginary world with little relevance to real life.

Keeping things in perspective, while we are always looking for explanations for what surrounds us, including giving meaning to our dreams, we keep in mind that dreams are unique. To interpret them effectively, we must place them in the context of our own experience and reality. No one else can have exactly the same background, emotions, or experiences as anyone else.

So please be cautious when trying to discern the meaning of your dreams or of anyone else's. Seek guidance from an expert such as a psychoanalyst, because dictionaries or interpretation books are only guides that may not lead you to fully understand what you know best: yourself.

13

SUNDAY NEUROSIS:
THE GLOOMINESS OF SUNDAYS

Imagine waking up one morning after a hectic work week with a strange feeling of confusion, as if you have no idea what day it is or what you need to do. You slowly sit up and realize that it's Sunday. You feel disoriented, lacking energy, and unsure of what to do. What is causing this? Throughout the week, your mind has been focused solely on work, and now you find yourself with free time and no plans; you experience a sense of "fear of emptiness" that leads you to ask, "What am I doing? "Where am I going?"

Experiencing a sense of emptiness from having nothing to do on a weekend, after a hectic workweek, can indicate something deeper than mere boredom such as some kind of existential crisis and a lack of meaning to life.

This sense of emptiness can also occur during the vacation period, when some people may experience feelings similar to those of certain retirees, who may find themselves overcome with uncertainty about how to fill their time with so many "days off". This can result in feelings of sadness and depression. Have you ever found yourself in a similar situation?

The lack of activity can be challenging for some people, as they are accustomed to long workdays, high levels of stress, and packed schedules. The sudden lack of routine, both physically and mentally, that occurs when people are suddenly given a couple of days off during the weekend, with "nothing to do," is a challenge that can disrupt their accustomed routines.

Some people claim that after a hectic pace throughout the week, where they typically sleep an average of four hours each night, they should ideally enjoy their Sundays. However, this can lead to feelings of frustration and a lack of direction, as they struggle to find ways to fill their time. Some assert that Sundays, which should be a day for rest and recreation, leave them feeling unfulfilled and even depressed without knowing why.

This state of being was described by Viktor Frankl, the Viennese psychologist, we discussed in a previous chapter as "Sunday neurosis".[37] It is characterized by a sense of existential emptiness and a significant imbalance between professional and personal or family life. Frankl identified that people experiencing these feelings lack a deep and transcendent sense of purpose in their lives, which is why they feel terrified and experience a strange nostalgia when Sunday arrives, prompting them to pause their daily tasks and confront their own selves with fear.

On the other hand, there are those who seek total escapism through entertainment. You've probably come across the unfortunate incidents that occur when young people engage in risky behavior, such as driving under the influence of alcohol or drugs, or driving without a seatbelt. These incidents often result in serious injuries or fatalities.

The majority of these incidents are caused by speeding, alcohol consumption, or the use of illegal drugs. In his book *"Psychoanalysis and Existentialism"*,[38] Frankl analyzes these behaviors and comments that many times the phenomenon occurs in people who are unaware of the purpose of their lives and whose individual identity lacks transcendent meaning. Such people tend to live in the fast lane, never having had the opportunity to identify who they are, why they exist, or what is their mission in life. In these modern times, a considerable proportion of the population is dominated by irresponsibility, apathy, and boredom.

In the absence of a clear sense of purpose, they attempt to fill their lives with a high level of activity and constant stimulation, even if it's all about scrolling endlessly on their social media apps. While they may work or study diligently from Monday to Friday, when the weekend arrives, they tend to exhibit obsessive and frenetic behaviors. In this weekend neurosis, there is a tendency to engage in a wide range of activities, including alcohol consumption, drug use, and sexual promiscuity. These behaviors are often undertaken with the intention of having fun and clearing the mind. And ultimately, these behaviors are designed to provide a temporary escape from reality and to facilitate the ostensible pursuit of happiness.

The key issue is that happiness, the feeling of being satisfied with oneself, can never be the direct result of a search for meaning. Rather, it is the consequence of having found a purpose to live for.

Many people aspire to achieve happiness throughout their lives. However, the act of obsessively pursuing it can actually prevent them from being happy, as the more they seek it, the further it recedes.

Humans have become conformists (following the lead of others) or totalitarians (following the directives of others), which has led to a state of tedium and boredom. Sometimes, the sense of existential emptiness is masked by the pursuit of power, wealth, or pleasure. However, even with these masks, the deeper sense of emptiness often remains. Therefore, Frankl proposes that we re-examine the fundamental values of being human in order to give our lives a deeper and more transcendent meaning.

Some suggestions for your consideration are:

• Find a balance between work and family life by organizing work and family activities in an agenda or calendar, allocating specific time for each. It is also necessary to engage in entertainment, recreation, sports, and hobbies.

• Set aside quality time for personal life, family, and friends to strengthen bonds. In addition, couples should set aside time for themselves.

• Visit a relative, friend, or acquaintance who lives alone or is ill.

• Contribute to the community; engage in activities that benefit others. Volunteer your time, get involved in community events or donate money or goods.

• Remember that personal development is very important, so it is wise to devote time and resources to yourself (in activities such as reading, meditation, or exercise).

It is necessary to properly delineate the spaces of work and leisure, family and personal development, as they are complementary elements that give a more transcendent and profound dimension to our existence; in this way we are more likely to find what can contribute to giving a fuller sense of meaning to our lives.

(14)

ME, MYSELF, AND I

Have you ever experienced that when you meet with a friend, they immediately start talking about themselves, their life, their adventures, and their misfortunes, as if what happens to them is the only interesting thing in the world? Or when you want to talk about your problems and concerns, that friend becomes impatient for you to finish so they can continue their endless monologue that starts, continues, and ends with "me, me, me"?

Self-help books and motivational authors emphasize the importance of self-valuation and the enhancement of abilities. However, some individuals go beyond self-evaluation and define themselves as "the best at something" due to their achievements, skills, or capabilities. In their interactions, they tend to be self-absorbed and believe that only those with similar levels of intellectual ability or comprehension can engage with them on their level. They always prioritize their own characteristics over those of others and make negative comments about individuals who achieve success.

Many artists, politicians, intellectuals, and television presenters came to mind who fit perfectly into the description above. These individuals seek recognition from others and have an exaggerated ego. However, these behaviors are not exclusive to celebrities.

It is normal for everyone to have traits that can be perceived as selfish by others to some extent. This does not necessarily indicate a significant issue. Certain behaviors or attitudes may manifest in a mild manner. The issue with individuals who have an exaggerated ego is not that they are exceptional, but rather that they have a strong sense of self-worth and believe they are superior to others. Those who exhibit an exaggerated self-love are often referred to as *narcissists*.

The term "narcissism" has its etymological origins in Greek mythology. Narcissus was a very attractive young man. Despite the admiration of the maidens, Narcissus was uninterested in reciprocating their feelings, which resulted in their disappointment. In punishment for Narcissus's vanity, the goddess Nemesis made him fall in love with his own reflection in a pool of water. Narcissus was unable to look away from his reflection, and unable to touch or embrace it. He eventually drowned himself in the water. Following Narcissus's demise, a beautiful flower grew where his body fell, and from that point forward, it was known as Narcissus.

Narcissism is a personality disorder, and there are various subtypes. Each of these subtypes has distinctive characteristics that would require an entire book to fully explore. Here we will focus on the general traits associated with overt or grandiose narcissism, which is the "classic" type.

Narcissistic individuals are characterized by a sense of grandiosity, which manifests as an overvaluation of their abilities and an exaggeration of their knowledge and qualities. They tend to be boastful and require constant admiration and attention. Consequently, they may be surprised if they do not receive the praise they believe they deserve.[39] If they achieve success in sports, business, or any other area, they are proud to flaunt it to others, demonstrating their superiority. They even anticipate being received with fanfare and are taken aback if others do not envy their possessions or achievements.

In essence, narcissists believe others envy them because they themselves covet others' successes. They believe they are more deserving of achievements, admiration, and privileges. However, beneath their apparent overestimation of these accomplishments lies a lack of confidence and a low self-esteem.

In individuals with narcissistic traits, self-esteem is expressed in an exaggerated manner, with a tendency to seek the "best" or the "most important" in any given situation. For instance, they frequent the most exclusive restaurants and educational institutions, reside in the most sought-after neighborhoods, drive the most luxurious vehicles, and wear the most expensive apparel and accessories. Their inflated sense of importance leads them to believe that they cannot associate with just anyone; they feel they must seek out people of their own caliber. As a result, they frequently brag about having the best doctors, lawyers, politicians, and athletes among their friends.

Narcissism is a mask that conceals a person who feels less valuable than they appear. In other words, the narcissist unconsciously uses mechanisms to defend themselves from reality and unwanted conflicts through high self-esteem.

It is typical for narcissists to live in an alternate reality, one filled with fantasies and a sense of power over others. Their self-perceived entitlement leads them to believe they deserve special treatment, which in turn makes them appear arrogant and haughty, while also making them insensitive to the needs and desires of others. For instance, they frequently believe that they should not have to wait in line at the bank or that their priorities are so important that others should cater to them.

For the narcissist, a friendship or romantic relationship is only possible if the other person is willing to fulfill their desires. Due to their self-centeredness and focus on their own needs, they are unable to empathize with others and therefore fail to recognize others' feelings and needs. In conversation, they make exaggerated hand gestures, speak loudly, and appear disinterested in what others say. If a colleague or employee is experiencing a challenging situation, they may not be receptive to listening to their concerns because they are not genuinely interested in their well-being. However, if the narcissist themselves feels upset, they will seek support from others.

In the most extreme cases, narcissists end up alone because they tend to be rejected by those around them when they become unbearable. In such instances, they seek new contacts who admire them, although over time, they will again face rejection.

Additionally, narcissists tend to resist suggestions and corrections from their partners or colleagues. They are also reluctant to accept advice, as they believe they already know everything and therefore do not need it.

Furthermore, narcissists often adopt a defense-oriented

posture, exhibiting highly sensitive responses to the actions and comments of others.

But then again, not only high-profile athletes, artists, entrepreneurs, or individuals with the highest number of followers on social media can develop these behaviors. It could also be your neighbor, your boss, your friend, or even yourself. It is therefore important to consider some guidelines to avoid engaging in behaviors that may be harmful to oneself and those around you:

- Be respectful and accept that others have their own ideas and capabilities that entitle them to express themselves and participate in the discussion.
- Learn to listen to others, engage in conversation in a way that makes the other person feel their thoughts are important, and acknowledge that you can learn from them.
- When offering constructive criticism to someone who might be a narcissistic individual, it is important to do so in a delicate and sincere manner. A spoonful of honey helps the medicine go down.
- In the most severe cases, it may be necessary to seek professional help to develop the necessary skills to interact in society in a more appropriate and sincere manner.

Having a positive self-esteem and an awareness of one's personal strengths and attributes should not lead to a desire to be the center of attention.

15

CAN YOUR MIND MAKE YOU SICK?

According to data from the World Health Organization (WHO), over 800 million people worldwide (approximately 12% of the global population) allocate at least 10% of their family budget to healthcare for themselves, their children, or other sick relatives. But did you know that a high percentage of the illnesses we suffer have no medical explanation and are due to psychological causes?

Let us take a look at Carlos, who works in an office normally for eight hours a day. His boss is unpredictable, however, and sometimes demands that he stay late to handle the backlog. To get home, Carlos has to drive for over an hour in heavy traffic, and when he arrives, his young children are already asleep. He often argues with his wife and feels stressed all the time. For a little over a month, he has been experiencing stomach discomfort, diarrhea and last week he was diagnosed with gastritis.

From a medical perspective, the cause of Carlos' discomfort lies in the consumption of alcohol, excessive spicy and fatty foods, a stomach infection, or the use of certain medications. From a psychological perspective, however, the negative emotions he is experiencing are causing physical symptoms in his digestive system. His body is expressing emotional distress through a series of symptoms.

The reality is that our bodies produce physical symptoms in response to emotions all the time. Do your hands shake when you have to give a presentation? Do you blush when you feel embarrassed? Do you get sick to your stomach after an argument? Your answer is probably "yes," because somatization is very common and is a physiological response to a psychological event. When we do not adequately manage our emotions, we can "somatize" them, that is, make our bodies sick.

Somatization is a set of physical symptoms that cause discomfort for which there is no identifiable physical cause. Illnesses known as *psychosomatic illnesses* can be caused by stress, emotional problems, or negative emotions, where internal psychological conflicts are able to manifest themselves physiologically.[40] Somatization is not a mental problem, but a consequence of the manageable relationship between mind and body.

According to the WHO,[41] the prevalence of diseases whose symptoms have no medical explanation is practically identical in almost all countries, whether developed or developing.

Psychoanalysis teaches us that when certain painful emotions become too intense and the distress becomes unbearable for the person, the tension is channeled outward; that is, the discomfort manifests in the body without having passed through the unconscious. [42]

Physical symptoms are generated, without a medical explanation, when we have high levels of stress or emotional problems that cause pain.

**The physical sensations that accompany
the emotions we feel are our body's own way
of warning us that something is wrong,
and they indicate what we need to do to regain balance.**

When we ignore or suppress what we feel and prevent tension from being properly expressed, it tends to accumulate. Then headaches, stomachaches, neck and back pain, sore throats, pharyngitis, chronic fatigue, asthma, allergies, and so on, appear.

The main causes of many of these primary psychosomatic conditions have been identified.[43]

- **Headaches:** Many people suffer from chronic headaches that are not due to a physical condition, but rather to a tendency to repress anger or frustration. The symptoms are a silent protest: when something upsets us or we dislike something but do not express it, headaches may occur. More assertive people experience less of this type of discomfort.

- **Back Pain:** Chronic pain in the back, shoulders, and lumbar region is very common and seems to be related to taking on too many responsibilities. The body experiences work or personal commitments as a heavy "burden".

- **Neck pain:** This type of discomfort is likely to be caused by a person, situation, or specific activity because it tends to be sudden. If we have a problem with someone or something we dislike, we may experience irritation or resentment, and certainly neck pain.

- **Sore Throat:** People who tend to suppress the expression of sadness experience a sore throat. By holding back natural crying, tension builds up in this area. A sore throat can also be caused by something we need to say but haven't expressed.

- **Colds:** While people often believe that exposure to extreme temperatures or rapid changes from hot to cold environments increase the likelihood of catching a cold, it's a fact that fatigue and stress weaken the immune system. Frequent colds have also been linked to feelings of sadness, disappointment, fear, or guilt.
- **Skin Problems:** Skin conditions and allergies seem to be a sign that there is some kind of problem in interpersonal relationships and in our interaction with our environment. They may be due to inadequate management of emotions such as fear, anger, and sadness.
- **Fainting:** Fainting, dizziness, fatigue, and similar symptoms are related to fear. When we feel that we don't have enough resources to face a threat, whether real or perceived, our body can become paralyzed.

What can we do to stay healthy?

We can't avoid physical symptoms in stressful situations, but we can prevent them from becoming physiological illnesses. We can learn to recognize them when they occur and change the way we respond.

First, it's important to consider that certain personality traits increase the likelihood of somatization. For example, highly negative and pessimistic people, as well as those who are depressed and anxious, tend to experience psychosomatic illness more frequently. Therefore, try to let go of negative emotions - such as resentment or anger - and learn to recognize them when they arise.

Instead of suppressing our feelings, we should share our

problems and worries with close people; it's even advisable to cry, as this helps us to relax. And, of course, it goes without saying that we should try to.

It's also necessary to avoid situations that cause us stress and discomfort as much as possible.

Changing our habits and lifestyle to include more physical activity and contact with nature is always very helpful.

Finally, listen to the sign your body is sending you and try to identify why you are feeling this way. The more attention we pay to these signs, as our external guides, the healthier our body will be.

16

STRATEGIES FOR CONTROLLING ANGER

Imagine any Wednesday, driving home after a day at work, slogging through city traffic with the "motivation" to get home to prepare dinner for the next day or do the laundry. Your boss scolded you for being late, didn't give you the day off you requested, and to top it off, you had to stay in the office during lunch to finish all your work. How do you feel?

The reaction may vary from person to person because we all have different ways of dealing with conflict. Most likely, however, anger would be your reasonable response to this situation.

Anger arises as a result of our discomfort when faced with adverse circumstances. When we cannot satisfy our desires or when we find ourselves in an unpleasant situation, we lose control. This discomfort turns into anger, rage, and even hatred, making us increasingly uncomfortable and restless. It can even prevent us from sleeping, and even if we manage to sleep, we cannot rest.

One of the worst effects of anger is that we lose common sense, refuse to be reasonable, and desire revenge against those we believe have wronged us.

The most common reaction to a situation that doesn't turn out as desired expected is anger. However, it won't be a problem if we learn to control it and take advantage of an adverse situation rather than letting it control us and cloud our thoughts.

The first component that forms the chain of anger is our perspective on a particular situation: when we refuse to accept the fact that others see things differently and we cling to our blind belief that others should think as we do. If we are able to recognize these inappropriate thoughts before they turn into anger, it will be easier to control them, and we won't run the risk of suppressing our anger and letting it turn into resentment. This is why it's important to identify the mechanisms involved in anger.[44]

The foundational first component, as mentioned earlier, is thought: when we internally tell ourselves that others are trying to undermine us, that they are disrespectful. In response to this subconscious thought, a physical response occurs where our muscles tense up, our blood pressure begins to rise, and we prepare for the final stage - the attack - aimed at defending ourselves verbally or physically, hurting those we believe are hurting us first.

In this context, we might ask ourselves: Is it not valid to be angry and to want to be right? Are we going to let someone else get away with hurting us? Isn't it good to be angry, to express it, and not to let resentment build up? Doesn't conventional wisdom suggest that people who don't express their anger are more prone to health problems such as heart attacks?

Albert Ellis, a renowned psychotherapist and founder of Rational Emotive Behavior Therapy (REBT), mentions in his book *"Anger: How To Live With And Without It"*[45] that living in anger and fighting with others increases stress levels and heart disease. This is not to say that we shouldn't speak our minds or be honest. The point is that when we are angry, our vision becomes clouded and all the evidence seems to support us, validating our perspective even when it may not be accurate. When we're angry, it doesn't matter what others say because we tend to perceive deliberate aggression on their part.

Harboring anger toward someone usually results in constantly thinking about the hated person and investing a lot of time and energy in them. In addition, angry actions often create a vicious cycle of angry reactions.

When it comes to dealing with the problem of anger, it's common to hear various recommendations, such as punching a pillow to vent, yelling and complaining about how terrible things are, or writing down our feelings. However, Albert Ellis found that these methods of releasing anger only work temporarily. Therefore, he recommends fully and freely admitting that we hold grudges and resentments against others, but also recognizing that these resentments are created because we foolishly and unrealistically believe that others should treat us fairly and think the same way we do.

Below are some recommendations that will help you achieve effective anger management. If you practice them regularly, you will be able to control your emotions more effectively:

- Take a step back from the person you're angry with until your frustration eases a bit. When you feel calmer, express your anger, paying careful attention to the words you use.
- Write down the thoughts and ideas that come to mind about the person who upset you, and read them when you are calmer.
- Seek a solution to the problem rather than focusing only on what made you angry.
- Use first-person statements to avoid escalating tensions with others. For example: "I get upset when you ignore me."
- Practice relaxation techniques such as intentional breathing, visualizing a calming scene, or repeating a calming word or phrase.
- Try to be open to different opinions.

17

HOW TO MANAGE EMOTIONS

Everything in our lives involves feelings. Every event, no matter how simple, triggers a variety of emotions. Every memory rooted in our own personal history, or even that of our relatives is somehow associated with an emotional charge, because emotions are ultimately what keep us alive. An example of this is the heart, one of the most representative symbols across cultures throughout history, originally used by the Egyptians, who believed that the soul and spirit of man resided in this part of the body.

In Chapter 16 of this book, you read about the close relationship between thoughts and emotions. Many psychological problems result from an exaggerated emotional response combined with a distorted interpretation of reality. Often, we tend to suppress emotions, which, if not released, can lead to physical symptoms known as somatization.

The key to leading a healthy emotional life is to learn how to manage our emotions rather than suppressing them. Since it is not possible to stop feeling altogether, we can learn to manage our emotions through regulation. This involves learning a series of techniques that allow us to regulate our emotions so that we are not overwhelmed by them when negative events occur.

Emotions such as joy, sadness, surprise, fear, and anger can often take control of our lives without our conscious awareness or ability to manage them. However, by learning interact with your emotional states more effectively, you can achieve a healthier emotional life.

The following techniques are highly useful for managing emotions more effectively.[46]

Breath Control

There are various breathing techniques that can be used to relieve physical and mental tension. These techniques typically result in a greater sense of calmness by reducing stress, anxiety, and anger levels. There is a clear correlation between physical and mental relaxation and personal well-being, joy, and tranquility.

Deep breathing oxygenates the body and improves brain function, while simultaneously relaxing the body and mind. The majority of people tend to use shallow breathing and inhale through the mouth instead of the nose. Becoming aware of this helps us to practice a simple technique, as follows:

1. Inhale slowly through the nose instead of the mouth.

2. Breathe gently and deeply several times, keeping a rhythm. When doing this, the abdomen should expand as you inhale and contract as you exhale.

3. Take a couple of deep breaths through the nose followed by slow, gentle exhalations through the mouth.

To verify that you are performing this technique correctly, place one hand on your chest and the other on your abdomen and observe which one rises when you breathe. If the movement does come from the abdomen, then you are breathing correctly.

Thought Control

The first component of the chain reaction of negative emotions is the way we think about a particular situation. If we can identify and address negative thoughts before they escalate into anger, rage, or frustration, it will be easier for us to manage our emotions and remain in the driver's seat. And the first act of mitigation is to assess whether it is beneficial to become emotionally distressed in such situations. It is not productive to become depressed or annoyed when circumstances do not meet our expectations. The root cause of most emotional issues is our inability to accept reality as it presents itself. Rather than obsessing over our own sense of 'truth', evaluating our perspective leads to many more options and offers other approaches to interacting with the present moment.

The most effective method for identifying negative thoughts is to focus on the emotion that immediately follows the event. Imagine a discussion with your partner about which family to spend Christmas with. It is evident that the holiday season is a source of stress and conflict (in part due to family pressures), which can result in headaches and neck tension. These are clear indicators of an unpleasant emotional situation. However, it is not the discussion itself that causes the physical discomfort, but rather the thoughts that are associated with it: "I will not be attending my in-laws' house under any circumstances," "He is self-centered and only cares about his own family," "I always become ill when we spend the holidays with his family," and so on. It is not the disagreement itself that causes distress; disagreements are a normal part of relationships. Rather, it is how we think about the situation that causes distress.

Positive Affirmations and Thought Replacement

To fill our minds with positive affirmations, we must first eliminate negative thoughts. In the previous section, we discussed the importance of identifying which thoughts generate, prolong, or increase negative emotions, which can lead to feelings of sadness, anxiety, fear, or anger. Once these negative thoughts have been identified, they can be replaced with more positive ones. Being clear about which negative thoughts we wish to replace and what positive thoughts will substitute them empowers us with a clear mind about what we're trying to do. It helps tremendously to even write these down. Once this process is complete, the key is to implement it consistently so that a positive thought is automatically triggered each time a negative thought arises.

For instance, if you have weight issues, rather than thinking "I don't want to be fat," you should replace it with a positive affirmation such as "I am reaching and maintaining my ideal weight" or "I nourish and care for my body with healthy food and exercise." It is essential to have these positive affirmations in written form and to repeat them on a regular basis throughout the day. When practiced deliberately and repeatedly, they reinforce chemical patterns in the brain, strengthening certain neural connections and reducing anxiety.

Visualization

Visualization is an effective strategy for preparing ourselves for situations that make us feel insecure. This involves mentally rehearsing the feared situation, acting it out as if it were occurring in real time. Go as far as rehearsing the dialogues, movements, and scenarios while maintaining a positive mindset. As the number of visualizations increases, the level of anxiety decreases, and we become more comfortable and confident in our ability to successfully face the real situation.

For instance, if you are going to give a presentation, you should visualize every aspect of the situation and rehearse the dialogues while reinforcing your speech with positive affirmations. Once you have gained greater confidence, you may wish to practice in front of a mirror or record yourself on your mobile phone.

Although seemingly simple, these techniques described above are effective for effectively managing emotions. In addition to being used by psychologists and therapists, they can also be practiced by anyone who decides to turn them into a habit that allows for greater responsibility over emotions and feelings.

18

THE SHADOW EFFECT

Imagine this scenario: Your partner is a suspicious and insecure person who fears commitment and makes you feel like you are the one making things difficult in the relationship. Instead of accepting their problem of lack of trust, they unload their negative emotions on you and accuse you of being insensitive and selfish, attitudes they cannot accept in themselves. Why are they rejecting what is bothering them?

The German writer Hermann Hesse once said, "If you hate a person, you hate something in him that is part of yourself. What is not part of ourselves doesn't disturb us."[47] Through this mechanism, called *projection*, one person attributes their own feelings and / or thoughts onto another person's feelings, thoughts, impulses, or other behaviors that they, themselves, deny or find unacceptable within themselves. When we judge or criticize someone for being very arrogant, boastful, obnoxious, or selfish, we are actually, subconsciously, attributing to others the characteristics we detest in ourselves. Discovering in others the qualities we reject in ourselves is not an easy thing to admit, but it has a positive aspect, because without that person acting as a "mirror" of what we can't see, we would never have the opportunity to learn to recognize those qua lities in ourselves. Whatever we judge or condemn in others is ultimately a part of ourselves that we despise or reject.

Everything that irritates us about others can lead us to an understanding of ourselves. The general belief is that when we are critical of someone, we do so because there is an subconscious part of ourselves involved that we refuse to accept. In psychology, this subconscious aspect of personhood is called the *shadow*.

The physician and psychologist Carl Jung said that the shadow refers to the subconscious aspect of the personality, characterized by traits and attitudes that the conscious ego does not recognize as its own.[48] The shadow is everything we do not want others to see: the things we hide, the lies we tell, not only to others but also to ourselves. The shadow expresses itself in many ways: cheating on exams, drinking too much, eating chocolate cake when we are on a diet, yelling at our children or partners, cheating on our spouse, stealing ideas from our colleagues and claiming them as our own, etc. The shadow is made up of thoughts, feelings, and impulses that we find too painful or embarrassing to accept, so instead of dealing with them, we repress them.

How and when does the shadow arise?

The formation of our shadow occurs when we are children, before our minds are developed enough to filter the messages we receive from our parents. Some of these messages conveyed that something about us was not "good" and needed to be hidden: "How can you eat all this? "How can you wear that dress?" These messages, among others, may have sunk into our subconscious, altering our perceptions of our relationships and damaging our self-esteem.

None of us likes to admit that we have insecurities, so in order to hide them, we create an ideal persona at a very young age, thinking that this will bring us the attention, love, and acceptance we so desire. We wear masks of "kindness," "friendliness," or "sincerity" because we believe this will get us the affection and attention we crave. And while we put on these false masks and repress hatred, lies, shame, guilt, jealousy, or violence, all those parts of us that others and ourselves have judged to be bad or wrong, those parts cry out to be set free, accepted, and loved as valuable parts of who we are. Whatever we reject, we want to keep in the shadows, below our consciousness; we want to bury it.

You may wonder if it wouldn't be better to have no shadow and focus only on the positive aspects. Jung argued that everything that irritates us about others (and thus about ourselves) actually helps us understand ourselves better. Human experience is the result of the contrast between light and shadow, pain and pleasure; to manifest ourselves fully, we need these opposing energies. For Jung, every desire immediately suggests its opposite. When we have a positive thought, we cannot avoid having its opposite somewhere in our mind: to know what is good, we must understand what is bad, just as we cannot know what is black without knowing what is white. If we only knew goodness, truth, harmony, and the absence of everything contrary, there would be no creative impulse, just as there would be no creative impulse if we only knew the entropy of destruction or evil. Everything in life is based on pairs of opposites. When we reject our reality, we are fighting against ourselves.

Carl Jung said, "What you resist persists; what you accept transforms." In this sense, in order to live with our shadow and accept ourselves as we are, we must finger, re cognize and accept all the parts of ourselves that cause us pain. By becoming aware of them, a process of transformation begins.

How do we know if the behavior we detest in others is really our shadow?

If someone's behavior affects us emotionally and we overreact to it, we are probably projecting our Shadow. For example, if what you most dislike in others is hypocrisy, you may be confronting aspects of your own shadow, even if it's difficult to recognize. Of course, not everything we criticize or dislike is a projection of our own fears or shortcomings. However, a disproportionate reaction to something that isn't objectively very significant may indicate that something has been triggered in our subconscious.

19

GHOSTING

When my friend Sofía broke her leg, she spent a lot of time at home and became addicted to the Internet. She started opening accounts on all the popular social media platforms, and with her eloquence, it wasn't difficult for her to make friends. With her first virtual boyfriend, she exchanged text messages, emails, and later long phone calls that made her think the relationship was getting serious.

A few weeks later, the person in question stopped contacting her, so Sofía began harassing him with WhatsApp messages that were never answered. Her trip to the city where he lived was in vain, as she only discovered that he had moved.

After getting over the grief of her failed relationship, she met a new prospect who lived in another country. Shortly after they met, he traveled to the city where Sofía lived to meet her. For a whole week, my friend devoted herself wholeheartedly to her new love, but as soon as he returned to his country, he stopped contacting her.

Has it ever happened to you that after meeting someone, exchanging phone numbers, spending time together, and even starting a relationship, everything suddenly stops? This situation corresponds to a phenomenon known as *ghosting*,[49] where overnight the other person simply stops responding to your messages or calls, blocks you from their social media profiles, and disappears from your life without any explanation. In other words, they end the relationship by simply disappearing, like a ghost, without giving any reason, leaving the other person wondering what went wrong.

Although ghosting has become more common, especially with the rise of new technologies, it's not a new phenomenon. In the past, people used to wait by their landlines for their partners to call, assuming that the call must have come while they were out of the house. I remember one of my teachers in high school, a very intelligent and kind woman in her fifties, who told us the story of her youthful love, a Russian man with whom she corresponded for a few years until one day he simply disappeared and she never heard from him again. In her effort to maintain an idyllic memory of their failed relationship, my teacher used to say that she had always suspected the man was a spy, forced to distance himself from his loved ones to avoid endangering them because of his dangerous job.

In the age of apps like Tinder, OkCupid, or Match, it's much easier to reduce people to a "profile," which makes them easier to ignore because there's not the normal empathy that comes with meeting someone in person. Blocking or ignoring someone has led to an increase in the number of people experiencing ghosting because it requires very little commitment.[50] Those who ghost want to let the other person know that they no longer want to continue the relationship, but they act cowardly and avoid having a conversation. On the other hand, the victim tries to rationalize what happened by considering all the possibilities: maybe they lost their phone, maybe they had an accident, maybe they are busy at work, or they have personal problems... They cling to a minimal and unrealistic hope that the "ghost" will still call. As days go by and the truth is revealed without any justification, the person who has been abandoned shows frustration at being left with many unanswered questions and a clear sense of discomfort, since even a minimal explanation would have made them feel respected.

What to do if you're a victim of ghosting?

Since ghosting is a reality and will continue to become more common, it's best to confront it. If you notice that the other person is starting to withdraw, be brave and ask them directly if everything is alright, so that the conversation can lead to them opening up about their feelings.

On the other hand, avoid harassing the "ghost" with messages and phone calls, as Sofía did. If they don't respond, stop writing or calling; you're dealing with someone who doesn't respect you enough to give you a reason to end things. Someone who leaves without explanation isn't worth it.

Also, stop feeling guilty about experiencing ghosting. Trying to figure out what went wrong won't bring the "ghost" back; in fact, their reasons for disappearing probably have nothing to do with you and everything to do with themselves. Even though it's a thoughtless act, avoid giving it any more importance and just accept that the other person doesn't want to communicate with you.

**Don't let your feelings overwhelm you.
It's normal to feel sad and angry for a while,
but obsessing over a failed relationship
won't do you any good.**

Finally, remember that what's important here is your healthy perspective and how you can remain responsible for your own feelings. So take care of yourself and invest your time in people who make a positive contribution to your life.

20

TALKING ABOUT SEXUALITY
WITH CHILDREN

Do you remember how scared you were when your son or daughter first asked you where babies come from? Were you able to give an adequate answer, or did you get nervous and respond with the classic story of the stork that came from Paris, the egg that mommy laid, or the little seed that daddy planted in mommy? Today's children aren't easily satisfied with the answers our parents gave us in the past. Children are eager to know, and with technological advances, they increasingly have access to a wealth of information, much of which may not be the most appropriate.

Talking to children about sex is one of the most difficult topics for parents. Often, parents feel prepared to explain to their children how to use a cell phone, but struggle to discuss fundamental personal development issues such as sex. Their curiosity about sex may be triggered by Internet use, friends, the presence of a new baby in the family, or when they feel their privileged position is threatened by the arrival of a new member at home, such as a sibling, toward whom they may begin to show hostility, seeing them as a rival for parental affection. In this sense, they ask: "Where do babies come from?" or rather, " Where does the intruder come from who is going to take away my privileged place at home, and what must I do to prevent this from ever happening again?".

In these cases, it's best to answer their questions as they arise and in a natural way, because it has been shown that children who are better informed make fewer mistakes in their relationships and value affection more.

Many parents believe that giving children too much information can lead them to their first sexual experiences. However, research confirms the opposite: children who have more information from an early age make better decisions about sexual matters.[51]

"Where do babies come from?
How did I come out of your belly?
Why do boys pee standing up but girls sit down?"
Hearing these and similar questions from children
should not be a cause for alarm, but rather
an opportunity to prepare appropriate answers
that provide them with reliable, first-hand information.

How to respond to questions about sexuality[52]
The first thing to consider is to answer naturally, just as children ask: be honest, be truthful to avoid confusion. If we don't want children to lie, adults shouldn't either. Questions should be answered directly, using language that children can understand and without long explanations that might

confuse them. Of course, how you answer will depend on the age of the child. For example, a two-year-old may be satisfied with answers such as "You grew in Mommy's tummy" or "Mommy and Daddy made you," and may go on with his or her normal activities for months or even years without asking further questions. However, if a four- or five-year-old asks why his or her mom or neighbor has a big belly, it might be a good idea to explain that a baby grows inside, in a kind of sac called a "womb," and that this happened when two cells (seeds) from mommy and daddy came together to form a baby.

It's okay if parents don't know how to respond or get nervous when their child asks an unexpected question. Questions are not exams to be passed, and the only way to learn how to answer questions about sexuality is to discuss the topic.

It's important to note that children get information from many sources, but information about sexuality is the responsibility of parents, not the Internet, friends, or teachers. Therefore, you should not be afraid to discuss sex with your children, and you should certainly not delegate it to others, who may offer inaccurate information.

Avoiding discussing sex until puberty is even more delicate. For many children, it is too late to discuss sex with their parents once they reach puberty, when they are often reluctant to do so because they are embarrassed to share something so private that they might have already experienced without their parents knowing.

In conclusion, it's not a matter of discussing sex with children at a specific age or at a specific time, but of doing so naturally from the beginning. It's also not advisable to "bombard" them with information about sex at any time, but rather when they show interest and in terms they can understand. It's important to give children the confidence to keep asking questions; if they are reprimanded for asking "indiscreet" questions, they may not dare ask their parents about such an important topic ever again.

Finally, teaching moral values at an early age will help children understand that sexuality is also about feelings and affection, for oneself and for others.

21

WHAT ARE YOU AFRAID OF?

Do you feel paralyzed when you have to speak in public? Do you feel it when you see a spider? When you walk on a bridge? When you enter an elevator? When you are in the dark?

It's normal to feel anxious when we find ourselves in circumstances such as these. We've all experienced scary situations, such as taking a math test in school or walking past a growling dog on the street. In most cases, fear is adaptive, because the anxiety it brings motivates us to learn new ways to face life's challenges.

However, there are people who find it impossible to control their fear; they become paralyzed and experience a variety of physical reactions: body tremors, rapid heartbeat, sweating... and an urgent need to escape from their immediate environment. This type of response is called a phobia.

A phobia is not just any fear, but an extremely intense feeling toward a specific situation. It is also a type of anxiety that does not go away: someone who suffers from a phobia will not experience fear once or twice, but every time they see or face whatever it is that triggers the phobia, and they will try to avoid it at all costs to avoid feeling threatened.

People who suffer from phobias develop certain tactics to reduce their fears. However, these tactics are always uncomfortable and do not eliminate the fear; they only mask it to prevent people from confronting the object that causes their aversion.

The Diagnostic and Statistical Manual of Mental Disorders (DSM-5) defines a phobia as a clear and persistent, excessive and irrational fear triggered by the presence or anticipation of a specific object or situation, such as insects, heights, or fear of flying.[53]

A person with a phobia does not need the presence of the object or situation they fear to experience tension or discomfort. Simply imagining the event associated with their fear can cause strong psychological and physical reactions. This is evident in the case of Ivan, one of my patients with a fear of flying (*aerophobia*): "I'm afraid of flying, that's why I stopped flying. In fact, I changed jobs because I used to travel a lot. When I could, I traveled by car, but sometimes the distances were too long and it was impossible. Days before the trip, I would start to feel terrified, have nightmares about flying, and feel extremely anxious. When the plane door closed, I felt terrible, trapped. My heart would start pounding and I would sweat a lot. As the plane began to climb, the feeling of not being able to escape tormented me as I imagined losing control and going crazy. I wasn't afraid of the plane crashing or the turbulence; it was just the feeling of being trapped. The last few times I flew, I took a sedative and even mixed it with alcohol. It helped me calm down, but I didn't want to get addicted to substances and I didn't want to go through the whole process every time I had to fly, so I quit".

Often a phobia can be traced back to an intense fear experienced in childhood. For example, a child who never learned to swim and who vividly remembers his desperate attempts to stay afloat may continue to be terrified of a shallow pool as an adult. However, if the intensity of the feared stimulus is low, people with phobias generally do not experience symptoms.

According to the DSM-5, diagnosing a phobia involves evaluating avoidance, fear, or anxiety related to the phobic stimulus. This is especially important if these reactions significantly interfere with the person's daily activities, work, and social relationships, or if they cause obvious distress.

When a person encounters the phobic stimulus, he or she immediately experiences anxiety. This reaction can sometimes escalate into a panic attack, accompanied by symptoms such as shortness of breath, nausea, fainting, dizziness, fear of dying or losing control, increased heart rate, and feelings of suffocation.

It is estimated that 9% of the world's population suffers from some form of phobia, making it the most common mental disorder after depression.[54]

Phobias can be grouped into five major categories:
- Animals (fear of rats, snakes, insects, etc.).
- Nature (fear of heights, water, storms, etc.).
- Blood, injuries and surgery.

- Environmental Circumstances (fear of crowds, traveling alone, public transportation, elevators, bridges and tunnels, etc.).
- Social situations (fear of being around strangers, speaking in public, being watched while eating, etc.).

Although many of the situations we fear do not pose a real danger, phobias can seriously affect our lives, so it is important to address them.

Phobias do not usually go away on their own, so it is important to seek help. Today, there are several treatments available to help those who suffer from phobias. However, before starting any treatment, a phobia must be diagnosed by a professional (psychologist, psychiatrist, or doctor) to avoid confusing a phobia with an anxiety disorder or another medical condition.

Specific phobias are often treated with psychotherapy, which helps patients understand the reasons for their fears and trains them in techniques (such as controlling breathing and muscle tension) to manage anxiety when faced with the situation that triggers their fears.

Cognitive-behavioral therapies combine a series of strategies to overcome phobias, such as exposure to the stimulus, systematic desensitization, and restructuring of thought patterns.[55]

In Iván's case, the first goal was to understand the nature of his fear, why it occurred, and what triggered it. Subsequently, the situations that caused him anxiety when flying were identified, ranging from the least to the most distressing. He was then taught breathing and relaxation techniques to manage anxiety. He also participated in visualizations and flight simulations, where he practiced the techniques he had learned. This gradual preparation led to a real flight, where he applied what he had practiced. Initially, it was difficult, and he felt fear, but gradually, the fear diminished, and Ivan managed to overcome his fear of flying. The key to his success was to stop avoiding his fear and to have the will to face it.

22

DO YOU HAVE A PHONE ADDICTION?

Do you feel anxious when you realize that your phone has no battery or that you left it at home? When you don't have your phone with you, do you think about the number of calls and messages you're missing? Do you stop any activity when your phone vibrates, signaling a new message? Do you get up in the middle of the night when you get a WhatsApp message? If you answered yes to any of these questions, you should definitely read on.

Since the advent of smartphones, most people spend many hours a day connected to their phones, whether checking social media or browsing the web, making this habit a necessity. As a result, some people feel completely "lost" when they find themselves without communication.

Despite the fact that technology is very useful because it allows us to stay connected at all times and have instant access to information, being disconnected can have a negative effect, causing a sense of anxiety similar to that caused by psychotropic substances.

The anxiety and obsessive-compulsive symptoms that some people exhibit when they are without their cell phones have been the subject of a thorough study by psychologists, who have named this irrational fear *nomophobia,* the fear a person experiences when leaving home without their phone.

Nomophobia is an abbreviation of "no-mobile-phone phobia," a term coined during a study conducted by the Royal Mail to gauge the anxiety of mobile phone users. The study, which surveyed 2,163 people, found that 53 percent of respondents experienced anxiety when they lost their phone, ran out of battery or credit, or had no coverage.[56] Among the most common reasons for anxiety were feeling "isolated" from potential calls or messages from family and friends, and work demands that require constant connectivity. In addition, the research showed that the stress level of a person with nomophobia is comparable to the anxiety experienced the day before a wedding.

According to statistics, smartphone users check their phones an average of 34 times a day, but when they are unable to check their messages or calls for any reason, people with nomophobia experience anxiety, increased heart rate that physicians call tachycardia, obsessive thoughts, and headaches or stomachaches.[57] In addition, higher blood pressure, neck pain, and feelings of "hurt and alone" have also been reported as symptoms by addicted individuals.

The level of dependence on the cell phone for those experiencing these symptoms ranges from using it as an indispensable tool for basic tasks like waking up to satisfying important needs like feeling safe and connected to the world.

Some people report sleeping with their phone at night like a teddy bear, while others consider the phone an extension of themselves and their identity: their most precious possession.

According to experts, cell phone addicts tend to be insecure individuals with low self-esteem who lack social skills and spend their free time on their phones without really enjoying it. People with this addiction often find it easy to make friends in cyberspace, but struggle to connect in real life.

Although this disorder is more common among teenagers, who have a greater need for acceptance from others and are more familiar with new technologies, it also occurs in high percentages in the adult population. It has been found that women suffer from this disorder more than men because their brain structure requires a greater need for communication and affection.

What can we do to reduce our dependence on our phones and the time we spend with them? Here are some tips that can help:

- Get rid of your postpaid plan and switch to a prepaid plan. By controlling the number of megabytes you use, you'll be able to better monitor the time you spend on your phone.
- Turn your phone off an hour before bed.
- Uninstall unnecessary applications and games that make you waste time on your phone.
- Access websites through the browser, as it is usually less engaging than the app, which is designed to "trap" you for longer.
- Disable app notifications to avoid checking your phone frequently.
- Don't take your charger with you when you leave the house; you'll have to learn to use apps, messages, and calls properly or your battery will die.

- Resolve to check social media only once or twice a day, in the morning and at night.
- Just as you take a break from work and study on weekends, try to avoid using your smartphone on Saturdays and Sundays.
- During your "dead time," read a book instead of checking your social media.
- Go on a "diet" to check your phone less often each day and engage in other activities as a form of therapy.

In 2014, one of the pioneering programs to treat technology addiction took place in Japan.[58] A dozen teenagers spent eight days in the forest, where they hiked and engaged in other outdoor activities, cooked their own meals, and participated in cognitive-behavioral group therapy with three psychologists. During this time, the teens were not allowed to use their cell phones. The goal was to treat the symptoms of smartphone addiction they exhibited, such as attention deficit, hyperactivity, anxiety, depression, sleep disturbances and, in some extreme cases, social phobia. Although the teens were initially reluctant to engage with the psychologists, by the end of the program they were much more outgoing and talkative.

Therapy has been shown to be effective in addressing online compulsions, and effective therapy focuses on helping individuals recognize their compulsion and regain control over their use. Techniques include interval training to delay responding to notifications, and reducing app use to promote healthier habits.

In the end, successful recovery from compulsive online and smartphone use requires more than just behavioral change. It requires a profound shift in an individual's relationship to their digital habits.

23

THINGS YOU SHOULD KNOW
ABOUT AUTISM

According to the World Health Organization (WHO), one in every 160 children has an autism spectrum disorder (ASD).[59] It occurs in all racial, ethnic and social groups and is four times more common in boys than in girls. Epidemiologic studies conducted over the past 50 years suggest that the global prevalence of the disorder has increased.

The understanding of autism has evolved significantly in the last 17 years. In 2007, Ban Ki-moon, Secretary-General of the United Nations, stated that people with autism possess a wide range of abilities and have different areas of interest, but they all share the ability to make the world a better place.

The Diagnostic and Statistical Manual of Mental Disorders (DSM-5)[60] includes "autism spectrum disorder" among neurodevelopmental disorders because it typically manifests early in development, often before school age, and is characterized by deficits that impair personal, social, academic, or occupational functioning.

It's called a "spectrum disorder" because people with autism can exhibit a wide range of symptoms. Some may have difficulty speaking and may not make eye contact when spoken to. They may also have limited interests and repetitive behaviors. They may spend a lot of time repeating a phrase over and over (appearing to be in their "own world").

Characteristics of Autism Spectrum Disorder

The main diagnostic criteria for this condition include:

- Persistent deficits in communication and social interaction. Autistic children may show indifference to people or focus intensely on one object for long periods of time to the exclusion of others.
- Abnormalities in eye contact and body language. The child may not respond to his or her name and often avoids eye contact with others; there is also a complete lack of facial expression and nonverbal communication.
- Difficulty making friends, lack of participation in social games, and a preference for solitary activities.
- Lack of interest in other people: The inability to develop relationships with peers (including siblings) hinders the development of shared interests or goals with others, resulting in a lack of social or emotional reciprocity and a disregard for the needs of others.
- Repetitive patterns of behavior, interests, and activities: Lack of typical spontaneous and varied play or imitative play appropriate to the child's developmental level.
- Insistence on sameness: Autistic individuals exhibit restricted, repetitive, and stereotyped patterns of behavior, activities, and interests, often showing a strong attachment to unusual objects. For example,

they may repeatedly arrange a toy in the same way, take the same route to school, rock or spin themselves, etc. They may also exhibit self-destructive behaviors such as biting or hitting themselves.

- In young children, there may be an inability to hug, indifference or rejection of affection or physical contact, and an inability to respond to a parent's voice.
- Hyper- or hypo-reactivity to sensory stimuli: An autistic person may show apparent indifference to pain/temperature, adverse reactions to sounds, excessive sniffing or touching of objects, and visual fascination with lights or motion.

The exact causes of autism spectrum disorder (ASD) are not well understood. Research suggests that both genetic and environmental factors play a significant role in the development of ASD.

Autism can be diagnosed early, typically by the age of three. Parents are often the first to notice their child's unusual behavior. For example, they may describe how the child seemed different from birth, or in other cases, how their development progressed normally to a point where it not only stopped, but regressed, resulting in a loss of skills.

It's important to determine whether the child has autism and to rule out intellectual disability without autism, hearing impairment, or other language and learning disorders in order to provide appropriate treatment.

Unfortunately, there is no cure for autism spectrum disorder. All therapies focus on reducing symptoms and improving the patient's quality of life. There are ways to maximize a child's ability to grow and learn new skills.

The earlier the child receives help, the greater the likelihood of a positive impact on symptoms and skills. Treatments include behavioral and communication therapies, skill development, and medication to manage symptoms.

Some research has shown that individuals with autism may benefit from animal-assisted therapies, such as those involving dogs and horses.

Temple Grandin, one of the first autistic people to document the insights she gained from her personal experience with autism, is a prominent author and speaker on both autism and animal behavior. Grandin is a consultant to the livestock industry, where she offers advice on animal behavior. She is also an internationally lauded autism spokesperson, and one of the best examples of how people with autism can benefit from animal-assisted therapies.

In the late 40's, when Grandin was two years old, she was formally diagnosed with "brain damage". From the age of two and a half, she received personalized training in speech therapy, as well as all kinds of occupational therapy and educational games that helped her develop. As a teenager, she spent a summer vacation at her aunt's ranch in Arizona. There she realized that animals, like her, had emotional problems, and she told herself that she had to learn how to help them, so part of her therapy involved riding and caring for horses.[62]

Her interest in animals led her to observe that cattle calmed down when placed between two metal plates that squeezed the cattle on their sides, and she came up with the idea of creating a similar "hug machine" for herself that would give her the tactile stimulation she so desperately needed but could not get because she could not stand physical contact with people.

One of the best-known methods of enabling children with little or no language to communicate is PECS (Picture Exchange Communication System),[63] which allows individuals with limited or no verbal skills to communicate using pictures. A child or adult with autism can use PECS to communicate a need, a thought, or anything that can reasonably be shown or symbolized on a picture card. In more advanced stages, users are taught to respond to questions and make comments, and some people who use PECS also develop speech.

Although it is common for autistic children to require support throughout their lives, there is a significant percentage of autistic people who are able to develop independent personal and professional lives, or with minimal support.

$$24$$

ENGINEERED SHOPAHOLISM

Have you ever wondered why products you didn't include on your shopping list, such as chocolates, candy, magazines, batteries, and chewing gum, are placed right next to the checkout counter where you usually stand in line?

It's very common for supermarket advertisers to use various strategies that directly target our subconscious minds to make us spend more without our rational minds noticing. In this chapter, we'll explore some of the psychological tricks supermarkets use to get us to spend more.

The color associated with discounts

Red is often used to draw attention and convey urgency, which is why it's common to see signs in stores advertising clearance sales, even though it doesn't always mean the product is below its original price. Along with red, orange is often used to draw attention, such as product labels and shelf tags advertising a discount, because it combines the energy of red with the cheerfulness of yellow.[64]

Fruits and vegetables first

Fresh fruits and vegetables are usually placed near the entrance of supermarkets because, on a subconscious level, they give us a sense of relief by getting the healthy items first. This allows us to add less healthy items to our cart later without feeling guilty.

Aromas that trigger hunger

Another common tactic in supermarkets is to place bakeries or food sampling stations in strategic locations in the store where the smell of freshly baked bread reminds us of a favorite bakery from our childhood. The sight of a delicious-looking product activates our salivary glands, further triggering our desire to consume that food.

Basic product proliferation

Have you noticed that staples such as eggs, milk, meat, and bread are scattered in different areas of the store so that you have to walk between them as much as possible? In addition, milk, meat and cheese are located in the back of the supermarket. By forcing you to cross the store to find what you need, you're likely to walk past countless specials and tempting displays, leading you to buy products you didn't intend to buy.

Shelf placement

Products that sellers want us to buy are placed at eye level so we can easily see them before we see other perhaps less profitable items. On the other hand, less expensive products are usually placed on the bottom shelves so that we don't pay as much attention to them, since the seller hopes that we'll be satisfied by what we see first. Candy, on the other hand, which is very appealing to children, is placed on the lower shelves at children's eye level so that they can convince their parents to buy it. Since most of us are right-handed, we tend to buy products on the right side, which is where the more expensive products tend to be.

The big shopping cart

Most supermarkets use large shopping carts to make us feel like we haven't bought enough, which encourages us to fill them up.

The power of music

Music has been shown to have a significant impact on our behavior. In supermarkets, slow music relaxes shoppers and subconsciously encourages them to stay longer; the longer we stay, the more we spend. So effective is this kind of mindless music found everywhere in our shopping experiences that an entire industry has been created for this demand called "Muzak".

Reorganization

Although supermarkets don't regularly change the location of products, they do periodically change the placement of sections, forcing us to walk through aisles and shelves we don't normally pass until we find the product we're looking for. In this way, we discover (and hopefully, for the store, buy) products we hadn't noticed before.

Large retailers invest million$ in carefully planned marketing campaigns to increase sales, taking advantage of psychological motivations of which we are often very unaware.

The size of the supermarket

It has been shown that when we are in crowded places, we tend to get stressed and shop faster, resulting in a lower total purchase. Conversely, when we can shop more leisurely, we buy impulsively and fill our carts more. So the bigger the stores, the more time we spend in them.

Prices ending in 9

This is perhaps the oldest and best known trick because we tend to focus on the first digit of a price and not think in terms of cents. Thus, a product that costs 9.99 registers in our minds as nine dollars, even though its actual value is almost one dollar more than we originally calculated. In this way, we spend more without fully recognizing it.

How to protect yourself

Despite all these efforts of retailers to lure us into making bigger purchases, we can still protect ourselves. The first thing you should do is plan your shopping with a list and stick to it. Have a budget in mind and don't go over it; if possible, bring only cash to avoid the temptation to buy more. Try not to use a shopping cart, but rather a basket or just your hands, so that you buy only what you need. Finally, don't go to the supermarket when you're hungry because you'll end up buying more than you need and even more than you want.

25

PSYCHOLOGICALLY COLORFUL

Have you ever wondered what the Coca-Cola logo would look like if it wasn't red? Have you ever imagined the Facebook logo in orange? Or the Starbucks logo in brown? Colors evoke emotion, and brands use them to drive purchases through recognition and loyalty.

Colors are very important in all aspects of our lives because they influence our mood and the image that people, companies, brands and products project.

It's no coincidence that most health-related companies, such as toothpaste brands, use white and blue; that brands or companies dedicated to ecology and recycling are green; and that milk cartons at the supermarket are white.

It has been proven that shoppers often choose what to buy based on color.

According to the Color Marketing Group, a company that specializes in the use of color, color accounts for about 85 percent of the reason a person chooses one product over another.[65] Each color conveys a sensation and a meaning, and our response to it is a mix of instinctive mechanisms handed down to us via various forces of social and cultural learning;

for example, we associate pink with girls and blue with boys. Let's consider some examples of what colors mean and which ones are most recommended depending on their use and context.

You may have noticed that restaurant chains like McDonald's or Pizza Hut use red in their logos and interiors. This is because red quickly attracts attention, evokes strong emotions, and increases appetite. Red also symbolizes passion, energy and intensity, evoking emotions such as love and danger. Red lipsticks are mostly red, and basically the purpose of wearing red lipstick is to increase sex appeal, since lipsticks try to emulate the physical state of sexual arousal.[66] As a very intense color, red has negative effects when we try to perform tasks that require concentration, such as taking an exam or making a decision, as it increases blood pressure and muscle tension. In addition, red is often used by large stores to mark sale tags and stimulate the urge to buy. Red is also synonymous with trust and security, which is why many insurance companies and banks use it, such as Santander, Scotiabank and Mapfre.

On the other hand, yellow is considered a cheerful and warm color, but its use is more complex because it can cause eye fatigue. Companies such as Amazon, National Geographic, Best Buy, Sabritas and Hertz use it in their logos because its positive qualities include raising alertness and conveying clarity.

Blue inspires peace, relaxation, and wisdom. Unlike red, this color lowers blood pressure and breathing rate. It is widely used by water brands, and because it is associated with cleanliness and health, it is often found in surgical attire. In the world of marketing and business, blue is very popular because it conveys security and is not aggressive. American Express, Ford, Facebook, Skype and Dell are some of the many companies that use it.

On the other hand, orange is synonymous with enthusiasm, excitement, warmth and caution. That's why it's used to attract attention and evoke joy. In the world of digital marketing, it's used to encourage shoppers to take action through buttons like "buy," "sell," or "subscribe". Companies like Amazon, Home Depot, Mastercard, Hooters, Aljazeera Firefox, and, of course, Orange, formerly known as France Télécom, as well as products like Fanta or Crush are widely known for their use of orange.

Green is associated with health, calm, money, and nature. It's been proven that people who work in environments dominated by green tones are more relaxed. Brands such as Holiday Inn and Starbucks incorporate these colors into their logos to leverage green's association with relaxation.

Black, white, silver and gold tones are generally used for luxury items because they convey sophistication and rarity. Brands such as Prada, Michael Kors and Chanel use them for this reason.

White is also associated with purity, innocence, and openness. In addition, this color is ideal for making small spaces feel larger.

Finally, pink is a color associated with femininity and romance. It is used to attract the attention of women and is also associated with intimacy. Brands such as Victoria's Secret use these attributes in their branding.

After learning about the reactions each color evokes, you may be wondering how you can use color psychology to benefit yourself at home and in the office. In the office, blue is recommended because it is associated with productivity and focus. In the bedroom, it's better to use green because it promotes calm, a sense of health, and aids in sleep. For the kitchen, yellow is a good choice as it brings brightness, light and energy to the space. In the dining room, red can be a good choice because it stimulates the appetite and passion.

Finally, if you have a shop or business, consider the type of product you sell and who will buy it; remember that blue is associated with water, green with nature and red with fire.

The most important thing is to clearly define what you want to convey when using color psychology in your personal life or business. Proper use of color will add significant value because it represents the essence of your personality and that of your brand or product.

26

DO SUBLIMINAL MESSAGES WORK?

In the 1960s, a famous experiment took place in a New Jersey movie theater. A tachistoscope - a machine used to project "invisible" messages on a screen that could be perceived by the subconscious - was used. During a movie, frames appeared with the following message: "Are you hungry? Eat popcorn. Are you thirsty? Drink Coca-Cola." According to the person who conducted the experiment, the results were astounding: sales skyrocketed.

Although the author of the study debunked the authenticity of the experiment years later, subliminal techniques were already widely used in advertising, raising concerns and imaginations of a world where people could be controlled by unseen advertising messages.

Are we really in the clutches of advertisers and their subliminal messages?

Today, it is possible to find subliminal messages on the web, in magazines, in supermarket advertisements, in late night television infomercials, and in self-help materials. But what are subliminal messages? How do they affect our minds? Do they really work? Let's delve deeper into these questions to get a better understanding.

First, it's important to mention that we have two ways of

perceiving reality: consciously and subconsciously. Conscious perception is well known: we see, hear, or feel something and process that information. Subconscious perception, however, is directly related to subliminal messages.

Subliminal means "below the threshold". The *threshold,* or *sensory threshold,*[67] is the limited spectrum where a diminishing stimulus goes from barely detectable to nondetectable; in other words, subliminal refers to what lies below the threshold of consciousness. When applied to a stimulus, it means that it is not consciously perceived but still influences behavior. But how much does it influence us? Well, if consciously we are able to process 50 bytes of information per second, subconsciously the speed increases to 11,000,000.

For example, if a high-speed image is inserted into a television commercial for a very short period of time, our conscious mind, which processes only 50 bytes per second, will not retain this information. However, to the subconscious mind, which processes at a rate of 11,000,000 bytes per second, this image will not go unnoticed. Therefore, a subliminal message is designed to be received by the person on a subconscious level without their awareness. It could be an image or sound that is transmitted so briefly that the conscious mind doesn't perceive it, yet it is stored in memory.

Subliminal content is used in some advertising messages to present a product or service to the consumer in such a way that the consumer feels a desire to acquire it without consciously knowing the authentic reasons for that desire. For example, advertising experts claim that the Coca-Cola glass bottle is shaped like a woman's silhouette to subliminally "capture" those who are sexually attracted to the female gender.

Psychology generally recognizes that much of our mental processing escapes immediate awareness and that we are unaware of many of our motivations.

Thus, much has been said about auditory messages recorded on albums by certain singers, some even claiming to contain satanic or suicide-inducing words. However, it has been found that these alleged messages do not persuade anyone when played at low volume within songs, or when contained in fragments that can only be understood when the recording is played backwards.

People do not change their behavior with auditory subliminal messages, so it is safe to listen to any musical group without concern. It has been proven that those who claim to hear satanic messages in commercials or music are allowing their heightened imaginations to seek out messages they are predisposed to perceive.

It's also important to recognize that much of what is called "subliminal advertising" is actually based on psychological conditioning associated with specific social situations. A classic example is tobacco advertising of the past, which often portrayed smokers as interesting, sensual, happy, and proud individuals in order to create the image that smoking would lead to romantic success.

In conclusion, it has not been proven that subliminal messages work to a significant degree. While some studies have shown that they can prime responses and stimulate mild emotional reactions in susceptible individuals, the consensus among scientists and psychologists is that subliminal messages do not produce a strong and lasting effect on a person's behavior. However, it's a powerful tool that's still used to tap into people's subconscious desires and get them to take specific actions, such as buying a product or service.

Therefore, you can rest assured that all the advertising around you actually has little real impact on your life and your buying decisions. Its effect on your mind is temporary, and the fact that the effect is not long-lasting may be one of its most successful attributes. Products change with fashions and times. A temporary effect seems to be exactly what marketers and advertisers want.

27

THE TRUTH BEHIND HYPNOSIS

Surely you have seen some show on television where a hypnotist, with the ability to control the will of dozens of people with a single flick of his wrist, asks them to do ridiculous things that the hypnotized later report that they do not remember. How much truth is there in that?

The shows where hypnosis is used to make someone lose control of himself thanks to the power of the words of a supposed hypnotist, and who wakes up at the sound of "one, two, three", are actually a farce, a trick that is very far from the method used by psychology and medicine.

Hypnosis or hypnotherapy is a scientifically supported technique that does not belong to the esoteric world or to witchcraft. Hypnosis is not a therapy in itself, but a therapeutic tool through which the psychologist helps the patient to recall situations that he could not consciously recall.

Hypnosis uses guided methods of relaxation and intense concentration that allow the patient to focus their attention on achieving an elevated state of consciousness known as a *hypnotic trance*. During this state, contrary to what most people believe, we are not unconscious. During this process, brain activity is higher than when we are asleep, and we are aware of what is happening; that is, we are in a state similar to that of practicing yoga, relaxation, or meditation.

During hypnosis, the psychologist helps the person focus on specific information or concrete stimuli, such as their breathing, the therapist's voice, or a specific topic, while everything going on around them temporarily recedes into irrelevance for the person in a state of trance.

Although there are precedents for the use of techniques similar to hypnosis used by the Egyptians in their temples of sleep,[68] it was not until the mid-1800s that the first systematic study of a particular psychophysiological state, later known as hypnosis, began. The Austrian physician Franz Anton Mesmer is considered the father of modern hypnosis, having developed a theory about the ability of people to heal others through *animal magnetism*, or *mesmerism*. The development of Mesmer's ideas and practices led James Braid to develop hypnosis in 1842. In time, it was concluded that the "miraculous" healings in hypnotic trances, called magnetic sleep or mesmerism, occurred because of a condition known as *suggestion*.

Sigmund Freud, the founder of psychoanalysis, used hypnosis to work with forgotten traumatic memories that needed to return to consciousness in order to be healed.[69] Freud was the first to suggest that hypnosis could provide access to the subconscious, although he later replaced hypnotic regression with the evocation of memories expressed through words (free association) as a procedure for liberating the subconscious.

During a hypnotic trance, people can explore painful thoughts, feelings, and memories that they were unaware of because they were hidden in the unconscious (one of the systems of our mind that contains desires, instincts, and memories that we repress because they are unacceptable). Once the possible cause or psychological root of a disorder or symptom is explored and the trauma is revealed, the person can be referred to psychotherapy.

Hypnotherapy has been shown to be effective in treating depression, anxiety, gastrointestinal disorders, eating disorders, skin conditions, nausea and vomiting, childbirth, and chronic pain. In addition, hypnotic treatments can have long-term effects at a much lower cost than some traditional treatments.

Experts in cognitive science believe that since hypnosis has been used in the past to perform surgeries, amputations, and help people with severe pain, it is possible to use it today.[70]

However, hypnosis can be effective or ineffective depending on how susceptible to hypnosis or to suggestion a person is. The fact is that people vary in their ability to be hypnotized, so this procedure is not suitable for everyone and does not have the same effect on everyone. Between 10 and 15 percent of the population is "highly hypnotizable" and responds to almost any form of hypnosis, while about the same percentage of people is "poorly hypnotizable" and rarely, if ever, responds to hypnosis.[71]

In general, hypnosis should not be used on people with schizophrenia or severe mental illness to avoid exacerbating symptoms that are difficult to induce.

In conclusion, it is important to emphasize that hypnosis is not a dangerous procedure, nor is it brainwashing, as some people may believe, as long as it is performed by a highly qualified and authorized mental health professional.

28

THE FIRST IMPRESSION...
IS IT THE ONE THAT COUNTS?

Let's say you are going to meet someone, but you have to choose between two different personalities. The first is intelligent, hardworking, impulsive, critical, stubborn, and envious, and the second is envious, stubborn, critical, impulsive, hardworking, and intelligent. Which one would you rather meet? If your answer is the first, you are acting according to the majority.

In this experiment, originally developed by psychologist Solomon Asch in 1946,[72] the first person generally received more positive evaluations than the second, even though, on closer inspection, the adjectives used to describe them were the same, but in reverse order. In the first case, the positive adjectives are presented first, and these ideas influence how subsequent information is received, so that intelligence and being a hardworking person prevail over the other adjectives, which are perceived as relatively less important. Conversely, the person defined in the second description, with leading negative adjectives such as envious and stubborn, has the disadvantage that these characteristics overshadow the rest, rendering even the positive characteristics to be perceived as more negatively framed.

It has probably happened to you that when someone introduces you to another person, you are able to decide almost immediately whether you like them or not. Perhaps their appearance, tone of voice, or way of dressing makes you form a judgment about them in a matter of seconds and decide whether you like them or not. People often say that the first impression is the one that counts, but is that first impression always accurate?

We are all completely different and have traits that make us unique. When we meet someone, the first trait that catches our attention usually conditions what we think of that person and influences how we interact with them. If we start by describing someone's positive traits, they will leave a better impression, while if we start with their negative traits, they will leave a negative impression.

This cognitive bias is known as the halo effect and is very common in everyday life. This effect is an error associated with a lack of information when making judgments about circumstances or people, leading to exaggerations or understatements about abilities or attributes. In other words, an erroneous generalization is made based on selected characteristics or qualities of an object or person. The term *halo effect*[73] was coined in 1920 by psychologist Edward L. Thorndike as a result of his research with the Army. Thorndike observed that officers often gave others positive evaluations based on a single observed trait. Similarly, they generally ascribed negative traits to their superiors when they perceived an inadequate quality in them.

As can be seen, relying on first impressions can be dangerous because we infer characteristics based on limited information. For example, when we randomly identify the characteristics of another person, they may be influenced by the events of that day. That person may not be expressing their true self nor behaving in a way that more normally represents who they really are. If a person has had a bad day, our perception of them is likely to be different than it would be on one of their better days.

The halo effect is most obvious when it comes to physical appearance. When someone is perceived as attractive because of their physical features, they are also perceived as intelligent, successful, kind, and honest. In addition, recent experiments have found that attractive people are perceived to be happier, have a higher social and economic status, and come from better families than less attractive people. It's obvious that advertisements feature celebrities or famous athletes promoting products they have never used!

It is important to note that when we attach these "labels" to others, we do not do so with the intention of judging them prematurely; it is an adaptive resource that our brain unconsciously activates as a protective barrier to recognize what surrounds us and determine if it is safe and trustworthy. If the person or situation is perceived as threatening or dangerous, the immediate unconscious assessment leads us to react instinctively to avoid potential danger. The brain recognizes traits associated with past memories, and defensively leads us to prejudge. It's like meeting someone whose smile reminds you of someone who played mean pranks on you when you were a child. Then your brain activates defenses to protect you from getting hurt, even though the person you just met has no intention of harming you. However, as we have seen, the mind is not always accurate.

To avoid making false judgments, it helps to pay attention to information that confirms our first impression and to ignore information that does not confirm it, regardless of the order in which this information comes to us.

**It's easy to jump to conclusions and believe
that the first impression is all that matters.
This can make us irrational beings,
guided only by quick glances.**

We need an open mind and a deeper understanding of the other person, and we should treat the initial judgments we make about them as hypotheses, not absolute truths. While first impressions are important, they don't have to be definitive. The best part of getting to know someone is discovering what lies beneath the surface. And, the efforts we learn to make in this direction bring about our own self-development as a rewarding byproduct.

29

HOW PREJUDICED ARE YOU?

"Blue is for boys and pink is for girls," "Men should work and women should stay home and take care of the children," "Men shouldn't cry," "Women can't do heavy work," "Soccer is for men," "Blondes are stupid," "Dolls are for girls," "Fat people are nice," or "Women can't drive.

No doubt you have heard phrases like these on more than one occasion, or perhaps they are even part of your usual repertoire. You may have used them for some time without realizing that they are stereotypes, passed from mouth to mouth, and not necessarily true.

Making prior judgments (prejudices) about a situation or a person is inevitable because we have all been raised with certain beliefs and values. But what happens when these beliefs turn into unfair generalizations? Do you know how to recognize them and let them go?

Stereotypes are opinions about the characteristics (traits and behaviors) attributed to a group; that is, they are organized beliefs or ideas about the characteristics associated with different social groups, such as physical appearance, interests, occupations, nationality, gender, and so on. We learn and assimilate these ideas, which have been socially transmitted to us over generations, and we assume them to be true. This leads us to make general statements, whether positive or negative, about a particular group. For example, it is often assumed that women do not have the ability and disposition to hold leadership positions, even though they have demonstrated that they have the same abilities as men to hold high positions and lead teams. In fact, in many cases, they have demonstrated much more effective leadership than men in various areas or disciplines (for example, we could cite the few female leaders around the world who demonstrated quick and timely handling of the health crisis in their respective countries during the Covid-19 pandemic: Taiwan, Germany, New Zealand, Finland, Iceland and Denmark).[74]

But not all the interpretations we make tend to be negative. A stereotype can be positive or neutral; for example, Japanese people are generally thought of as hardworking and disciplined. However, it is more common to highlight negative stereotypes, such as the misconception that women are not good drivers.

Where do these stereotypes come from? Mainly from the upbringing we receive at home. The family is our basic reference point, the place where we learn the rules of beha vior, habits, values, and forms of communication that allow us to relate to others. The models that our parents, grandparents or aunts and uncles teach us become the attitudes and behaviors that we later adopt, and many of them are based on stereotypes and prejudices that do not correspond to reality.

Stereotypes often create prejudice because they espouse sometimes irrational assertions empowering us to form a judgment or opinion without having enough information to support it in an objectively rational way.

Prejudices are generally negative thoughts and attitudes that an individual has toward another person or group of people. They are an unjustified reaction to a person based on his or her membership in a particular social group. Prejudices are opinions that are accompanied by feelings or emotions, usually negative. While stereotypes are essentially beliefs, prejudices are attitudes related to stereotypes; that is, they have an emotional component.[75] For example, if you travel on public transportation and clutch your purse when you see a man with tattoos, you are acting on the erroneous and stereotypical belief that men with tattoos are dangerous. If you did not have the reaction of grabbing your bag to avoid theft, your behavior could simply be stereotypical, but the inclusion of an emotional component (fear) makes it a prejudice.

There are many prejudices. Let's consider just a few: all Muslims are terrorists; people from low socioeconomic backgrounds are the ones who steal; the French are unfriendly; women don't know how to drive; men are insensitive; homosexuals are a bad influence on children; Catholics are fanatics; and all politicians are corrupt.

Prejudices go beyond simply categorizing people because they condition our interactions with them. Stereotypes block our critical faculties and cause us to adopt prejudicial attitudes that can lead to practices of discrimination and intolerance.

Of course, the line between stereotypes and prejudice is not always clear. In fact, it is difficult to perpetuate stereotypes without expressing some form of prejudice, especially when the stereotypes are perpetuated across generations. Perhaps the most negative consequence of the existence of stereotypes is the creation of negative prejudices that lead us to hate groups of people simply because they carry a label. The case of the racial hatred that drove the Nazis to kill millions of Jews or the Rwandans to exterminate each other between Tutsi and Hutu tribes are the clearest examples of what prejudices can do.

At some point in our lives, we have all felt entitled to judge others based on the way they dress, the color of their skin, the way they act, the way they speak, or the way they think. These prejudices do not benefit us or those targeted by them, especially in a society that is becoming increasingly intolerant and tends to criticize everything in a negative way. Some have even coined the phrase, "Cancel Culture". Although we may have been taught to judge others throughout our lives, it is possible to change these thoughts and behaviors and turn them into positive actions.

Here are some steps we can take to do so:
- Let's keep an open and flexible mind to avoid false prejudices.
- Take time to observe a person or group carefully before acting impulsively or "labeling" them.
- Avoid jumping to conclusions when encountering a new person or group.
- Show empathy for those we have been taught to judge in order to avoid being judged ourselves.

- Be open to new knowledge and groups of friends to broaden our understanding (each person is unique, regardless of the group in which we find them).
- Remember that prejudices exist in everyone's mind, so we must eliminate them there.

30

SIMPLE WITNESSES

A middle-aged man stands in line for the subway and watches a pickpocket in action broad daylight. The thief steals the wallet of the woman in front of him and walks away without her noticing. Our protagonist clearly realizes that other people in the line also witnessed what happened. What does he do about it? The answer is: nothing. After all, no one else in the line reacted, so why should he? Pathetic, isn't it?

Now imagine that you were the one watching the thief in action. What would you have done? Would you have acted, or would you have remained a passive observer? The truth is, if you were in that situation, you probably would have felt socially constrained and done nothing either.

Are contemporary societies experiencing absolute indifference and a total lack of empathy? Do people only care about their own affairs without giving any importance to those of others?

The answers to these questions are not easy. It's not that the people in the subway didn't want to notice what the pickpocket was doing, or that they didn't have time to help, or that they simply didn't want to get involved. The reality is that if the subway station had been deserted, it would have been more likely that someone would have helped the robbed woman. But via a seemingly inexplicable silent consensus, the strangers in the subway formed a group with the rule "do not help".

Although it is stressful to see these kinds of situations where people are suffering or having a hard time and no one is doing anything to help, it is important to recognize that there are two conflicting rules at play here: one that says "we must help" and another that says "do what others are doing". So we have a group of strangers who subconsciously exert pressure on each other not to intervene.

What happened in this case is that the man was influenced by the apathy of the others in line: he was a victim of strong and subtle social pressure that prevented him from moving to act, even though he knew he should.

Now imagine that one of the people in the line decides to "rebel and disobey" the silent rule and goes after the pickpocket. Suddenly, more people would join the pursuit of the thief, forming a new group with the "help" rule.

The famous "Golden Rule" teaches us to do unto others as we would have them do unto us, and promotes a sense of community where everyone should help others if we want others to help us. However, this rule is often ignored because in various situations, people in need do not find the help they need because others pass by with indifference. This situation is known as the *bystander effect*.

In psychology, the *Bystander Effect* (also known as the Genovese Syndrome) is the name given to the phenomenon that the more people or bystanders present at a time, the less likely it is that a person in need of help will actually receive it.

The name Bystander Effect comes from a murder that took place in the United States in 1964. A woman named Kitty Genovese was returning to her apartment in a middle-class neighborhood. She was attacked and murdered with 17 stab wounds over the course of half an hour. Kitty screamed for help, and although police reports indicate that at least 38 people knew what was happening to Kitty or heard her screams, no one came to her aid. When the police asked the neighbors why no one had called them, the answer was that they thought another neighbor would have done it.[76] This event shocked people, and extensive editorials were published claiming that the United States had become a cold and uncaring society.

In 1968, the sociologists John Darley and Bibb Latané, concerned about the increase in the number of crimes committed in the presence of witnesses who did nothing to prevent them, conducted several social experiments. They concluded that when more people are present in a stressful situation, observers assume that someone else will intervene, and everyone refrains from doing so.[77]

If a person who is alone faces a problem, they will feel guilty if they do not act. But if others are present, the responsibility is shared because it is assumed that others will intervene to help.

When we think about it, we have probably all been passive bystanders in a stressful situation, even if it was not necessarily a crime as tragic as Kitty's. How many times has apathy prevented you from picking up the trash at the entrance to your building, reporting a water leak in your apartment, or helping a driver stranded on the road with a flat tire? The answer is simple: because you expect someone else to take the initiative.

It seems that by blending into the crowd, we avoid showing the feelings of empathy and altruism that we might show if we were alone in an emergency. All is not lost, however. Now that we know how the *bystander effect* works, we are better prepared to act and break the effect, both for ourselves and for others who observe without acting but more importantly, also for the victim in need. It is necessary to pay more attention to what is happening around us and to begin to engage with others. Stopping the mindset that what happens to others does not concern us is the first step to breaking the apathetic influence of others on ourselves. By forcing others to recognize that this is a situation that needs help, we will help them overcome the absurd thought that "if no one is doing anything, there is no need to do anything". It is important to accept that it is part of our nature to feel pressured by the group, but also to consider that we can become the "heroes" who break the habit of being mere spectators and encourage everyone around us to help.

31

DO YOU OVERESTIMATE
YOUR ABILITIES?

On April 19, 1995, in Pittsburgh, Pennsylvania, a man named McArthur Wheeler decided to rob a couple of banks in broad daylight without any protection or mask, allowing security cameras to capture him perfectly. When he was arrested shortly thereafter, Wheeler was surprised to be recognized and confessed that he had applied lemon juice to his face, believing it would make him invisible to the cameras. In his childhood, Wheeler used lemon juice to make invisible ink and write secret notes. Before the robbery, he had experimented with a Polaroid camera at home and noticed that his face did indeed not appear in the photos. What he didn't realize was that the stinging sensation from the lemon juice in his eyes had caused him to aim the camera slightly off, so his face was not captured by the camera.

This unusual incident led David Dunning and Justin Kruger, professors of social psychology at Cornell University, to question the unlikely story of the frustrated thief and to investigate the cause of his incompetence.[78]

Dunning wondered if it was possible that a person's own incompetence could make him unaware of it. To find out, he and Kruger initiated a study involving Cornell psychology students. The study consisted of asking each participant to rate their competence in the following areas: humor, grammar, and logical reasoning. They then took a written exam to measure their actual competence in each of these areas. The researchers then compared the results to see if there was a correlation. They found that the more incompetent a person was, the less aware they were of their incompetence, and the more competent and capable a person was, the more likely they were to underestimate their abilities.

The researchers published their findings in 1999 and named the phenomenon the *Dunning-Kruger effect*.[79] They pointed out that this unrealistic perception is due to the fact that the skills and competencies required to perform a task well are precisely the skills required to accurately assess one's performance on the task.

For example, if a person does not know how to park their car properly, the knowledge required to recognize that they are parking poorly and to correct it is precisely the driving knowledge they lack. They can only become aware of their inability to park well if someone else explicitly points it out, highlights their poor driving, and shows them the correct way to do it.

Additionally, an incompetent mind is not empty, but filled with preconceived ideas, intuitions, experiences, prejudices, hunches, and facts, as well as concepts borrowed from other fields of knowledge. With all this, it constructs stories and theories that give the impression of having reliable knowledge. In this way, a person is a victim of the Dunning-Kruger effect when boasting of being an expert in economics, for example, and believing that he has absolute and simple answers to the most important problems, but cannot implement a concrete proposal to generate economic growth.

Individuals who meet the criteria described by Dunning-Kruger also tend to be insulting and condescending, have poor reasoning skills, believe themselves to be great arguers, invent words because they consider themselves knowledgeable, accuse others of their own faults, and develop an exaggerated self-confidence. Those with this characteristic not only reach wrong conclusions and make poor decisions, but their incompetence prevents them from being aware of it.

Conversely, people who underestimate their abilities and competencies might do so due to the false consensus effect: they tend to think that "everyone does it the same way," assuming that their skills are average, even though their abilities are clearly superior. An exceptional driver, for example, might think that they only drive reasonably well because they believe it is something everyone does as well as they do.

The mistake of those who are true experts is not that they believe they know less than others, but that they often think others also know a lot about the subject they master.

We are all susceptible to experiencing this effect because we have incompetencies that we do not recognize. But if the Dunning-Kruger effect is "invisible" to those who experience it, what can we do to discover what we are doing wrong or to find out how good we are at other things? Here are some suggestions:

- Seek feedback from others and really consider what they are saying, even if it is difficult to accept. We should ask ourselves if we have heard similar criticisms or compliments from different people and ignored them.
- Acknowledge the possibility that we may not always be right and that we may need to acquire more knowledge in a particular area or come to terms with the fact that others lack the knowledge we have acquired in our areas of competence.
- Keep learning, because the more we know, the fewer "invisible" gaps in our knowledge we will have. Question what we know and pay attention to those with different points of view.
- Stay open to constructive criticism and resist the urge to become defensive, or as happens in some cases, to irrationally deprecate ourselves, perhaps to better fit in with those who might know less than we do.

Finally, always remember the old adage: "When confronted by a fool, it is better to remain silent and be thought a fool, yourself, rather than to engage and remove all doubt.

(32)

GENDER DYSPHORIA "EXPLOSION"

In February 2023, an article published in the New York Times related the story of Grace Powell, a transgender person who thought she was one during her teenage years, but no longer identifies as such.

Like many teenagers, Grace was uncomfortable with her body. She was unpopular in school and was bullied. Her adolescence did not make her feel better, as she suffered from depression and was in and out of therapy.

Influenced by online content and feeling "detached" from her body, Grace consulted a gender specialist and later, at the age of 17, underwent hormone therapy, followed by medications for gender reassignment. Before graduating from high school, she had a double mastectomy and began attending college as a transgender man.

According to Powell, at no point during her medical or surgical transition was she questioned about the reasons for her body discomfort, depression, or sexual orientation. Nor was she asked about previous trauma, so neither the therapists nor the doctors found out that she had been sexually abused as a child.

Grace, now 23, has stopped and reversed her gender transition (detransition) and admits, "The transition process didn't make me feel better. It magnified what seemed to be wrong with me." [80]

What Grace experienced in adolescence is known in the psychological field as gender dysphoria, a feeling of discomfort with one's gender.

Gender dysphoria occurs when a person's sense of belonging to one gender or the other, of being male or female, is at odds with their biological sex.

Gender dysphoria also means that the person experiencing it has a strong desire to get rid of their sexual characteristics, a desire to have the sexual characteristics of the opposite sex, and a desire to be the other sex and be treated as such. [81]

In the vast majority of cases, gender dysphoria appears in childhood, around 3 or 4 years of age, and in 80% of cases the distress disappears by puberty. [82] In the remaining 20% of cases, gender dysphoria persists into adulthood, and when it does, most professional approaches consider facilitating the transition.

When gender dysphoria first appears in adolescence, the risk of major problems is high because mental and psychological difficulties do not necessarily follow the onset of gender dysphoria, but may precede it. For example, it has been found that many boys and girls who develop this dysphoria have a history of psychiatric difficulties, especially autism spectrum disorders, anxiety, eating disorders, and depression. In these cases, experts recommend against gender transition.

Grace Powell began questioning her gender identity between the ages of 12 and 13. The fact that she did not experience gender dysphoria as a child and suffered from a mood disorder was ignored by specialists who believed: "There is one cure and one thing to do if this is your problem, and this will help you".[83]

Research shows that the clinical need for care of patients with gender dysphoria has increased significantly in recent years, and is much higher among women than men, although the reasons for this trend are not well understood. It is believed that significant advances in transgender rights, greater access to information, and better treatment have contributed to this increase.[84]

However, researcher Elisa Littman suggests that the explosion in the number of adolescent girls with gender dysphoria may be closely related to the dynamics of social contagion.[85] In her study, Littman found that parents described the onset of gender dysphoria in their children in the context of belonging to a group in which one, several, or even all of their friends experienced gender dysphoria and identified as transgender. Parents also reported that their children showed an increase in social media/internet use prior to revealing their transgender identity. In cases of late-onset gender dysphoria, that is, dysphoria that first appears during puberty or adolescence, researchers have questioned the role of social media in the development of gender dysphoria and of media exposure in increasing referrals to gender clinics.

The story of Grace Powell demonstrates how easily young people in this environment can be influenced by ideology.

In many cases, these are girls going through the normal identity and developmental issues of adolescence and are influenced to find a solution to their problems through transitioning.[86]

In the United States, the heated debate between those who want to help a growing number of children express what they have been led to believe is their wrong gender, on the one hand, and conservative politicians who "don't let kids be themselves",[87] on the other, has created a tense atmosphere and a sense that what should be addressed from a medical and psychological perspective has become a political issue.

Many who believe there should be a more cautious approach to treating gender dysphoria have been attacked as anti-transgender. Meanwhile, Gender-Affirming Treatment insists that doctors confirm the child's expressed gender identity and even provide medical treatment regardless of the child's age, and considers psychological intervention to explore other possible causes of distress as optional.

Based on widespread scientific evidence, care for individuals experiencing gender dysphoria suggests promoting desistance, which refers to the processes by which people stop pursuing medical transition and/or stop identifying as transgender.[88] Research supports promoting desistance until puberty, by which time gender dysphoria resolves in 80% of cases.[89] Psychological approaches should aim to address the distress caused by social rejection due to atypical gender expression. Interventions should also consider the children's social environment and emphasize family structure.

With respect to emphasizing the family structure, conversations between parents and children about gender should be encouraged, while exploring family dynamics, possible psychiatric histories of parents, and same-sex relationships of children. It is very important to develop and improve relationships between children and their parents, to avoid causing them shame and guilt, and to help them develop skills to cope with situations in which they may have a natural negative reaction to expressions of dysphoria. Children need help dealing with frustration, anger, and sadness caused by thoughts and feelings associated with gender dysphoria.

Transition should be considered a last resort, reserved for cases where dysphoria persists into early adolescence and include a prepubescent history of clear and consistent expressions of dysphoria.

NOTES

---

[1] Erikson, Erik (1998). *The Life Cycle Completed*, W. W. Norton & Company.

[2] Castanedo, Celedonio (2008). *Seis enfoques psicoterapéuticos*, 2ª ed., El Manual Moderno.

[3] Lieberman, Charlotte (2019). "Procrastinar no es un asunto de holgazanería, sino de manejo de las emociones", *The New York Times*, March 26.

[4] Tony Robbins, https://www.tonyrobbins.com.

[5] Adaptación del test presentado por Davis, Martha y McKay, Mathew (1989). *Técnicas cognitivas para el tratamiento del estrés*, Martínez Roca, pp. 137-156.

[6] Davis, Martha y McKay, Mathew (2009). *Técnicas de autocontrol emocional*, Mr Ediciones.

[7] Goleman, Daniel (1997). *La salud emocional*, Kairós.

[8] Thomas H. Holmes and Richard H. Rahe, *Journal of Psychosomatic Research*, Volume 11, Issue 2, August 1967, pages 213-218.

[9] Filmaffinity (n.d.). *Falling Down*, https://www.filmaffinity.com.

[10] Encyclopedia Britannica (n.d.). "Catharsis", www.britannica.com.

[11] Cueli, José (1990). *Teorías de personalidad*, Trillas.

[12] Filmaffinity (n.d.). *Analyze This*, https://www.filmaffinity.com.

[13] Filmaffinity (n.d.). *Anger Management*, https://www.filmaffinity.com.

[14] Bushman, B. J. (2002). "Does Venting Anger Feed or Extinguish the Flame? Catharsis, Rumination, Distraction, Anger, and Aggressive Responding", *Personality and Social Psychology Bulletin*, https://doi.org.

[15] American Psychiatric Association (2014). *Manual Diagnóstico y Estadístico de los Trastornos Mentales DSM-5*, 5ª edición, Editorial Médica Panamericana, pp. 678-679.

[16] Martínez, Marcos (2018). "*Karoshi* o muerte por exceso de trabajo: cuando tu profesión genera adicción", https://hablemosdeempresas.com, May 29.

[17] Agencia EFE (2019). "Un 36 % de los empleados trabaja en exceso, según informe de la OIT", https://www.efe.com, April 18

[18] Frankl, Viktor (2003). *El hombre en busca de sentido*, Herder.

[19] CBC News. (2005). "Israelis receive organs from Palestinian boy shot by troops". https://www.cbc.ca/news/world/israelis-receive-organs-from-palestinian-boy-shot-by-troops-1.533038

[20] Frankl, Viktor (2003). *El hombre en busca de sentido*, Herder, pp.99.

[21] *Idem.*

[22] Filmaffinity (s. f). *The Glass Castle*, https://www.filmaffinity.com.

[23] Kornblit, Analía (2017). *Somática familiar: enfermedad orgánica y familia*, 2ª ed., Gedisa.

[24] Woods, Sarah (2019). "Bloodlines May Matter More Than Love When It Comes to Health", *Journal of Family Psychology*, November 7.

[25] Frankel, Richard (2017). "The Many Faces of Empathy", *Journal of Patient Experience*, https://www.ncbi.nlm.nih.gov, May 11.

[26] Sagi, A. y Hoffman, M. (1976). "Empathic distress in the newborn", *Developmental Psychology*, 12 (2), pp. 175–176, https://psycnet.apa.org.

[27] Rifkin, Jeremy (2010). *La civilización empática. La carrera hacia una conciencia global en un mundo en crisis*, Paidós.

[28] Carrillo, Sonia (2009). "Las campanas doblan por ti" de John Donne, https://hablasonialuz.wordpress.com, January 11.

[29] Filmaffinity (s.f). *After Lucía*, https://www.filmaffinity.com.

[30] UNICEF (2018). "Nuevos datos revelan que en el mundo uno de cada tres adolescentes sufre acoso escolar", https://es.unesco.org/news, October 1.

[31] Organización Mundial de la Salud (2013). "Informe de la OMS destaca que la violencia contra la mujer es 'un problema de salud global de proporciones epidémicas'", https://www.who.int, June 20.

[32] CFEC Estudio Criminal (n.d.). "El *ciclo de la violencia* de Lenore Walker", https://www.estudiocriminal.eu.

[33] Minder, Raphael. (2020). Ana Orantes, la mujer cuyo asesinato atroz hizo que España cambiara sus leyes. *The New York Times*, January 17.

[34] Freud, S. (2015). *La interpretación de los sueños*, Iberia Literatura.

[35] Filmaffinity (n.d.). *Spellbound*, https://www.filmaffinity.com.

[36] Barrett, Deirdre (2001). *The Committee of Sleep: How Artists, Scientists, and Athletes Use their Dreams for Creative Problem Solving—and How You Can Too*, Crown Books/Random House.

[37] Frankl, Viktor (2010). *Ante el vacío existencial. Hacia una humanización de la psicoterapia*, Herder.

[38] Frankl, Viktor (2018). *Psicoanálisis y existencialismo*, Fondo de Cultura Económica.

[39] Sarason, I. y Sarason, B. (2002). *Psicología anormal*, Prentice Hall Hispanoamericana, pp. 261-263.

[40] Real Academia de la Lengua (n.d.). "Somatizar", https://dle.rae.es.

[41] Pitt, Laura (2017). "Todo está en tu cabeza: por qué en un tercio de pacientes la causa de la enfermedad es emocional y no física", BBC Mundo, https://www.bbc.com, January 26.

[42] Heinrich, Haydeé (1996). "Neurastenia y psicosomática", Jornadas de la Escuela Freudiana de Buenos Aires, http://www.ef-baires.com.ar.

[43] Shapiro, Debbie (2011). *La conexion cuerpo-mente*, Ediciones Robinbook.

[44] Abrahms, Eliot y Ellis, Albert (2007). *Terapia racional emotiva*, Pax México.

[45] Ellis, Albert (2017). *Anger: How to live with and without it*, Citadel Press.

[46] Davis, Martha y McKay, Mathew (2009). *Técnicas de autocontrol emocional*, Mr Ediciones.

[47] Hesse, Hermann (2011). *Demian. Historia de la juventud de Emil Sinclair* (chapter 6, "Pistorius"), Alianza.

[48] Zweig, Connie (1993). *Encuentro con la sombra. El poder del lado oscuro de la naturaleza humana*, Kairos.

[49] Collins Dictionary (n.d.). "Ghosting", https://www.collins-dictionary.com.

[50] Samakow, Jessica (2014). "Ghosting: The 21st-Century Dating Problem Everyone Talks About, But No One Knows How to Deal With", HuffPost, https://www.huffpost.com, October 30.

[51] DiIorio, C.; Pluhar, E., y Belcher, L. (2003). "Parent-Child Communication About Sexuality. A Review of the Literature from 1980–2002", *Journal of HIV/AIDS Prevention & Education for Adolescents & Children*, Vol. 5, Issue 3/4, pp. 7-32.

[52] Stone, N.; Ingham, R. y Gibbins, K. (2013). "Where do babies come from? Barriers to early sexuality communication between parents and young children", *Sex Education*, 13 (2), pp. 228–240.

[53] American Psychiatric Association (2014). *Manual Diagnóstico y Estadístico de los Trastornos Mentales DSM-5*, 5ª ed., Editorial Médica Panamericana, pp. 197-202.

[54] Méndez, Fabiola (2017). "El 9% de la población mundial padece alguna fobia", UNAM Global, http://www.unamglobal.unam.mx, October 23.

[55] McKay, M. (1989). *Técnicas cognitivas para el tratamiento del estrés*, Martínez Roca.

[56] Cerda-Flores, R., *et al.* (2018). "Nomofobia en estudiantes de enfermería", *Revista Medicina de Torreón*, Volumen 9, Número 1, 23 de octubre, https://www.researchgate.net/profile/Ricardo_Cer-daFlores.

[57] Ayaquica, Jesús (2019). "Nomofobia: adictos al celular", UIC, https://www.uic.mx/nomofobia-celular, October 4.

58 Hermosín, Antonio (2014). "El *ayuno de internet*, remedio pionero para tratar la adicción a la red en Japón", ABC, https://www.abc.es, October 4.

59 Organización Mundial de la Salud (2019). "Trastornos del espectro autista", https://www.who.int, November 7.

60 American Psychiatric Association (2014). *Manual Diagnóstico y Estadístico de los Trastornos Mentales DSM-5*. 5ª ed., Editorial Médica Panamericana, pp. 50-59.

61 American Psychiatric Association (2014). *Manual Diagnóstico y Estadístico de los Trastornos Mentales DSM-5*, 5ª ed., Editorial Médica Panamericana, pp. 50-59.

62 Temple Grandin https://www.templegrandin.com/

63 Pyramid Educational Consultants. "El Sistema de comunicación por el intercambio de imágenes (PECS)", https://pecsusa.com-/pecs.

64 Colemans (2024). "The role of colour psychology in product labelling", https://www.colemanprint.com.au/blog/the-role-of-colour-psychology-in-product-labelling/.

65 Color Marketing Group (n.d.). "Identyfing color trends early", https://colormarketing.org.

66 Reynolds, Adrian (2024). "The Power of the Colour Red: Its Impact in Art and Design", https://adrianreynolds.ie/the-colour-red/.

67 Arellano, Rolando (2002). *Comportamiento del consumidor. Enfoque en América Latina*, Mc Graw Hill.

68 "La hipnosis en la época antigua" (2016), https://hipnotismo-blog.wordpress.com, December 25.

69 Cueli, José (1990). *Teorías de personalidad*, Trillas.

70 Blatchford, Emily (2017). "Hypnosis: Does It Actually Work?", Huffpost, https://www.huffingtonpost.com.au, August 22.

71 *Idem*.

72 Solomon, Asch (1946). "Forming Impressions of Personality", *Journal of Abnormal and Social Psychology*, 41, pp. 258-290.

[73] Thorndike, E. L. (1920). "A constant error in psychological ratings", *Journal of Applied Psychology*, 4(1), pp. 25–29, https://doi.org.

[74] Gómez, Ángela (2020). "Mujeres gobernantes que le atinaron al manejo de la pandemia", France 24, https://www.france24.com, May 12.

[75] Pico, Iván (n.d.). "¿Sabes las diferencias entre estereotipo y prejuicio?", Psicopico, https://psicopico.com.

[76] Manning, R., Levine, M. y Collins, A. (2007). "The Kitty Genovese murder and the social psychology of helping: The parable of the 38 witnesses", *American Psychologist*, 62, pp. 555-562, https://www.researchgate.net.

[77] Cieciura, Jack (2016). "A Summary of the Bystander Effect: Historical Development and Relevance in the Digital Age", *Inquires*, Vol. 8 (11), http://www.inquiriesjournal.com.

[78] Fehlhaber, Kate (2017). "La ilusión de la competencia", *Letras Libres*, https://www.letraslibres.com, 16 de julio.

[79] Dunning, David y Kruger, Justin (1999). "Unskilled and Unaware of It: How Difficulties in Recognizing One's Own Incompetence Lead to Inflated Self-Assessments", *Journal of Personality and Social Psychology*, 77(6), https://www.research-gate.net.

[80] Paul, Pamela. (2024). "As Kids, They Thought They Were Trans. They No Longer Do." *The New York Times*. https://www.nytimes.com/2024/02/02/opinion/transgender-children-gender-dysphoria.html.

[81] American Psychiatric Association (2014). *Manual Diagnóstico y Estadístico de los Trastornos Mentales DSM-5*. 5ª ed., Editorial Médica Panamericana, p.239.

[82] Feministes de Catalunya (2020). "Destransición de género. ¿Hay vuelta atrás?" [Video]. Youtube. https://www.youtube.com/watch?v=upJJhJmdSkM&t=5125s.

[83] Paul, Pamela. (2024). "As Kids, They Thought They Were Trans. They No Longer Do." *The New York Times*.

https://www.nytimes.com/2024/02/02/opinion/transgender-children-gender-dysphoria.html

[84] Ghorayshi, Azeen. (2022). "Report Reveals Sharp Rise in Transgender Young People in the U.S.". https://www.nytimes.com/2022/06/10/science/transgender-teenagers-national-survey.html.

[85] Littman, Lisa (2019) "Correction: Parent reports of adolescents and young adults perceived to show signs of a rapid onset of gender dysphoria. " https://journals.plos.org/plosone/article?id=10.1371/journal.pone.0202330.

[86] Gentleman, Amelia. (2022). 'An explosion': what is behind the rise in girls questioning their gender identity?" https://www.theguardian.com/society/2022/nov/24/an-explosion-what-is-behind-the-rise-in-girls-questioning-their-gender-identity

[87] Paul, Pamela. (2024). "As Kids, They Thought They Were Trans. They No Longer Do." *The New York Times*. https://www.nytimes.com/2024/02/02/opinion/transgender-children-gender-dysphoria.html.

[88] Clinical Advisory Network on Sex and Gender. (n.d). "What do the terms 'detransition' and 'desistance' mean?". https://can-sg.org/frequently-asked-questions/what-do-the-terms-detransition-and-desistance-ean/#:~:text=Detransition%20and%20desistance%20both%20describe,or%20stop%20identifying%20as%20transgender.

[89] Transgender Trend. (n.d). "Do children grow out of gender dysphoria?". https://www.transgendertrend.com/children-change-minds/.

THE AUTHOR

Blanca Pelayo holds a Bachelor's degree in Psychology and a Master's degree in Clinical Psychology and Psychotherapy from the Universidad Iberoamericana (Mexico). She has completed courses in addiction prevention, human development, and intervention for learning problems in children.

She has been in charge of the Psychology Department of the National System for the Integral Development of Families (DIF) and the Psychology Department of the Center for the Protection of Crime Victims of the Attorney General's Office in Puebla. She has worked in the diagnosis and treatment of behavioral and personality disorders, in crisis intervention with survivors of traumatic events related to violence, crime or accidents. She has also provided prevention and protection services for children against drug use.

She has worked as an academic director in private high schools, teaching general psychology, personality theories, psychopathology, psychological assessment, psychometrics, interviewing and psychological intervention.

Abroad, she has worked in institutions dedicated to the care of autism, the elderly, and the homeless.